FRONTIER FORTS OF TEXAS

Charles M. Robinson III

Lone Star Books
A Division of Gulf Publishing Company
Houston, Texas

Frontier Forts of Texas

Library of Congress Cataloging-in-Publication Data

Robinson, Charles, 1949-
  Frontier forts of Texas.

  Bibliography: p.
  Includes index.
  1. Fortification—Texas—Guide-books. 2. Texas—History, Military. 3. Texas—Description and travel—1981-   —Guide-books.   I. Title.
  F387.R65   1986   917.64 ′ 0463   86-10436

ISBN 0-88415-597-8

Contents

I
THE FIRST FORTS, 1

II
THE RIVER FORTS, 21

III
THE ADVANCING FRONTIER, 35

IV
THE CONQUEST OF THE PLAINS, 58

V
FORT SAM HOUSTON:
HEADQUARTERS,
DEPARTMENT OF TEXAS
U.S. ARMY, 71

VI
OTHER FORTS, 77

Acknowledgments

Any book of this type is the combined effort of many, many people. It is impossible to thank everyone, but here are a few who deserve special mention.

My wife, Perla. I don't have six pages for this, but basically for encouragement, proofreading, copying, and putting up with files on the floor of the living room for a year.

Tol Boswell, Jr., and Sam Penn Boswell of L. T. Boswell Ford-SAAB, San Benito, Texas, for arranging transportation on an extensive tour of Texas forts.

The Burnet Chamber of Commerce, for access to and information on Fort Croghan.

Robert Haynes and Jean Barnes of El Paso, for lavish hospitality and assistance in rounding up information on cavalry days and the Indian Wars in West Texas.

Robert Camina of Brownsville, Texas, for assistance with information on the closing days of Fort Brown.

My mother, Rosalyn C. Robinson, and my agent, Bertha Klausner, for their years of encouragement.

The Brownsville Historical Association, and to Henry Krausse and Bob Vezetti in particular, for access to military relics not normally available for handling by the public.

Nelson Bryan, editor of the *Whitney Messenger*, for material on the Fort Graham Restoration Project.

Jorge O. Gonzalez, Nuevo Santander Museum Complex, Fort McIntosh, Laredo, for invaluable assistance with background information and photographs.

The Management of Chadbourne Ranch, for access to the ruins of Fort Chadbourne.

Steve M. Elam, Merle Spaudling, Department of Parks and Wildlife, San Benito Public Library, William Lowe, Ivan Baker, Louise Smith and Lucia Fonseca.

Last, but not least, special thanks to Robert B. Dunkin, Rosa Luna, Gloria Martinez, and Frank Sanchez of the First National Bank of San Benito for their continued support, and more importantly, their friendship, as the bills on this project started to mount.

Preface

It has been more than 100 years since the guns of the last major military campaigns in Texas fell silent. The great wars of conquest and expansion taxed the energies and resources of five nations in succession for 150 years before the Victorio War settled the Indian question forever.

In the midst of these Indian campaigns, other races in the West and South went at each other four times—in the Mexican War of Independence, the Texas War of Independence, the Mexican War of 1846, and the War Between the States. Each of these battles relieved pressure on the Indians, allowing them to gain strength so that when these wars ended, the frontier had to be conquered again.

This book is an effort to describe the forts that held a key role in the Indian campaigns. And in telling of the forts, one must tell of the men who made them—of the battles, the suffering, the victories and defeats.

These days, with our twentieth-century sense of fair play, it is fashionable to feel sympathetic toward the Indians. So in some quarters, this book may be taken as chauvinistic. Certainly, the regular soldier serving on the frontier was no pillar of virtue, but neither was the Indian a noble child of nature. White and red understood each other only too well. And to see the situation as it really was, we must project ourselves back 125 years, into the mind of the Texas frontiersman living on the edge of Comancheria—one who might rise peacefully in the morning, not knowing if he would die hideously by nightfall. All too often he did die hideously.

This is the story of that period. And while it draws extensively on the work of others, the conclusions are entirely my own. For them I accept full responsibility.

No work of this type can claim to be complete. When I first started, I had planned to list every fort and to include points of interest and special activities centering around the various posts described. However, the list became so extensive that much had to be omitted. Therefore the reader might wish to use this guide as a companion to other Lone Star Books, including *The Alamo and Other Texas Missions to Remember*, *Backroads of Texas*, *Unsung Heroes of Texas*, and *Why Stop? A Guide to Texas Historical Roadside Markers*.

The book is arranged chronologically (and by extension geographically), beginning with the Spanish presidios and early forts. The next forts built were those constructed as defense against Mexican intrusion along the Rio Grande. As the Indians were pushed westward, the U.S. Army then strung a primary and secondary line of forts across the frontier. A whole section is also devoted to Fort Sam Houston, which served as headquarters for the Department of Texas, created when the Fifth Military District was divided. Forts and military camps that provide little interest for the visitor because of their location or lack of structures are listed in the final section beginning on page 77.

*Garryowen!**

Charles M. Robinson III

**The battle cry and regimental song of the U.S. 7th Cavalry.*

Fort Locations in Texas

Fort Elliott • (80)

• Fort Richardson (64)

Fort Belknap (41) •

• Fort Phantom Hill (43)

• Fort Griffin (67) • Fort Graham (80)

• Fort Chadbourne (78)

• Fort Bliss (32)

Fort Gates (80) • Fort Fisher (80)

• Fort Hancock (81)

• Fort Concho (61)

• Fort Parker (18)

Real Presidio de San Saba (14) • • Fort Croghan (39)

• Fort Quitman (84) • Fort Stockton (51)

Fort McKavett • (45) • Fort Mason (82) The Stone Fort (16)

• Fort Davis (53)

• Fort Martin Scott (81)

• Fort Lancaster (49) • Fort Terrett (84)

{ Fort Sam Houston (71)
The Alamo (3)
The Quartel de Bexar (8)

• Fort Leaton (81)

• Fort Clark (47)

• Fort Lincoln (81)

The Presidio La Bahia (8)

• Fort Inge (81)

• Fort Duncan (37) • Fort Ewell (80)

• Fort McIntosh (30)

• Uribe Home (84)

• Fort Ringgold (26)

Fort Brown (22) The Casa Mata (26)

(Numbers in parentheses are page numbers where the information on the forts can be found.)

Taming a Wild Frontier

The opening of Texas to American colonization brought a rapid expansion of settlement into the interior. Whereas the Spaniards had been content to settle around a series of missions and towns guarded by walled fortresses, the American colonists wanted lots of space in which to move about. This mobile society established the Republic of Texas, and kept its expansionist vision when Texas joined the Union.

However, the Texans' desire to settle where they chose, and to build new ranches and towns did not always coincide with the opinions of the natives. Comanches and Apaches particularly resented it. Already used to raiding Spanish and Mexican settlements, they viewed the lonely, isolated Texans as a whole new set of opportunities.

The Mexican War brought a chain of forts along the Rio Grande. So with the military already present, the next logical step was to build a new chain linking the Rio Grande with the Red River.

But United States military policy and Texas public opinion differed on the objective. At that time, Ohio and Minnesota were still considered the Western Frontier. The federal government's Indian policy was one of containment rather than suppression. This brought the Army into direct conflict with the Texans, who saw extermination as the only solution to the Indian question.

A change in federal policy came following the War Between the States, when Gen. W. T. Sherman barely avoided massacre en route to Fort Richardson. He agreed wholeheartedly with the extermination theory and brought an aggressive military policy aimed at ending the Indian trouble permanently. The frontier expanded rapidly after that, and within the next decade, the Indian question was settled forever.

Life on the Texas frontier was hard. Soldiers were often posted to lonely forts, away from water, hot and dusty in the summer and bitterly cold in the winter. Their forays against the Indians led to innumerable, forgotten battles, every bit as vicious and desperate as the more famous actions by Custer, Miles, and Crook. Often, the soldiers were hated by the very settlers they had been sent to defend, and they served on low pay, short supplies, and continual cuts in the military budget by a cost-conscious Congress.

In spite of it all, the average soldier did his duty. He won more often than he lost. And ultimately he opened and secured Texas so its citizens could live and travel in relative safety anywhere in the state.

I
THE FIRST FORTS

The earliest Texas fort of any significance was La Salle's ill-fated Fort St. Louis. This was built in 1685 on Garcitas Creek, inland from Matagorda Bay and consisted of some log cabins surrounded by a stockade. As we learned in our elementary school Texas history, La Salle left the fort and took some of his men on an overland march toward Canada. Somewhere near what is now Navasota, he was assassinated. Soon thereafter, Karankawa Indians overran the fort, massacred the men, and carried off the women and children. When Alonso de Leon found the fort in 1689, it was a scene of total desolation. Having no use for it himself, he burned it to the ground.

Were it not for the tragedy of the whole episode, the French effort in Texas would seem like a comic opera. Indeed, "Five Flags Over Texas" might be a more accurate phrase. As J. Frank Dobie once wrote, the French flag waved over Texas "tied to a pole in Louisiana."

But La Salle's expedition was important in one respect. A paranoid fear of France took hold among the Spaniards. Spain had discovered Texas in 1519 and had ignored it ever since. Now the threat of French intervention gave a sudden urgency to settling the vast province.

Early Spanish attempts at settlement came to nothing. Finally, in 1718, a settlement was founded on the San Antonio River, which somehow managed to hang on. Once San Antonio (or Bexar as it was then called) was established, colonization moved rapidly, if not always successfully. And with the colonists and missionaries came soldiers to protect them.

The Spanish language has many words to describe a fortified position. The one which concerns us is "presidio." Those presidios that have survived (two of them) were massive affairs, with barracks, chapel, and support structures surrounded by thick stone walls. These walls were capable of serving as gun platforms and had corner bastions to provide a better field of fire. Presidios were generally built as an adjunct to the missions, and were situated far enough away to avoid intimidating mission Indians, yet close enough to provide immediate military assistance, should the need arise.

While the missions might have relied on the presidios for protection, the missions, too, were built for security. The average Texas mission was surrounded by walls with rifle loops and bastions. It is no wonder the Alamo mission was adapted for military purposes by four different nations.

In areas where there were no soldiers, settlers would "fort up" inside a stockade or a particularly strong building, for defense against Indians and other marauders. An example of the pioneer stockade can be seen at Fort Parker, while the Stone Fort in Nacogdoches shows how a single building could be designed as a possible defensive point.

After independence, the government sought to establish a string of Ranger posts along the line of the frontier. But the Republic's shaky finances and other factors blocked full implementation of this plan. One of these Ranger forts has been reconstructed in Waco (see Chapter 6), but it is more significant as a modern repository of Ranger history and relics than for any part it played in the early days.

The frontier fort really came into its own after Texas was annexed to the United States. The American posts were simply a continuation of the Texas military tradition. To fully appreciate that tradition, it is necessary to see what existed for frontier defense prior to 1846.

The plaza of San Saba Presidio shows the sally port and ruined buildings.

The Alamo

On Alamo Plaza in San Antonio, about three blocks east of the Alamo Exit on I-35.

No other name in North America symbolizes heroism and grim determination like the Alamo. In the entire world, the desperate stand of 183 men under Lt. Col. William Barrett Travis has been compared to only one other event—the stand of Leonidas's Spartans at Thermopylae more than 2,000 years ago.

Yet that is only part of the Alamo's incredibly long record. It was built as a mission, but it served as a fort for Spain, Mexico, and Texas, a depot for the United States, an emporium and saloon, and finally a monument to Travis's heroes.

Early History

The order establishing the Alamo was issued on Dec. 28, 1716, by the Marquis of Valero, Viceroy of New Spain. The original is in the archives of the Franciscan College of Queretaro, in Celaya, Guanajuato, Mexico, and can be seen or even copied there.

With all the bureaucratic delays of Imperial Spain, the Mission San Antonio de Valero was not founded until May 1, 1718. The Presidio of San Antonio de Bexar and the town of Bexar were established four days later. The San Antonio Mission was what would one day become the Alamo. Initially it was named San Antonio for St. Anthony of Padua, and Valero for the Viceroy. The town and fort were called Bexar, after the Duke of Bexar, who had died in the Turkish Wars.

Shortly after their founding, the mission and fort were both relocated. Construction of the presidio around what is now the Military Plaza was begun in 1722. The plan shows a square with bastion points at each corner, similar to the Castillo de San Marcos in St. Augustine, Florida. There the presidio remained. But after a hurricane destroyed the huts which then made up the Alamo, a third move was made to its present site in 1724. From then on, the Alamo and the presidio were on opposite sides of the San Antonio River, and the town of Bexar grew up around the post.

By 1727, there were 273 Indians in residence at the mission. Work on a friary had begun, and the land around the mission was irrigated. The church was still temporary, but the overall situation looked good. Indians, particularly Apaches, harassed missionaries and soldiers on the trail, and a cholera epidemic caused many deaths. But the success of the San Antonio venture is evident from the help provided by mission Indians when the presidio and town were attacked by Apaches on the night of June 30, 1745. These hostiles had managed to set fire to the fort and were preparing to assault it from several directions when they were attacked from behind by Indians from the Alamo. The Apaches were routed and were actually chased some distance before the authorities called the mission Indians back.

Despite success, the San Antonio mission was hampered by lack of funds. It wasn't until 1744 that a permanent church building was constructed. This was a typical Texas mission chapel with vault, dome, and bell tower. However, workmanship was poor and the building collapsed within a few years.

Construction began anew about 1756 or 1757. This time, a master builder was put in charge. The church was apparently intended to be a masterpiece of mission architecture, with a large Baroque facade and two bell towers. Although never completed as designed, the walls have stood up for more than two centuries and are basically what we consider the Alamo of today.

The decline of San Antonio de Valero and other Texas missions came when the Spanish State began to distance itself from the Spanish Church. The Inspector General Teodoro de Croix visited Texas in 1777–78 and decreed that all unbranded cattle were to become state property. Since most mission wealth was reckoned in unbranded cattle, the missions found themselves penniless. They were no longer able to care for the large numbers of Indians congregated within their walls. After awhile, the mission Indians wandered off. Some married into the local population and settled in a squatter colony on the mission side of the river, which became known as La Villita.

At this time, the San Antonio Mission had a large enclosed plaza with Indian houses lining the walls inside. There was a fortified gate. The old granary in front of the convent was used as a temporary church. The convent itself surrounded a patio with a well. There was a walled backyard extending to the north. The unfinished church was to one side of the convent, outside of the main compound. This was essentially the arrangement that Travis chose to defend.

In 1793, the mission was suppressed and abandoned. However, in 1802, the old mission structures were taken over as a post for the Second Flying Company of San Carlos de Parras del Alamo, a cavalry unit sent from Parras del Alamo in Mexico. Henceforth, the mission would be known as the Alamo, after the soldiers. The company stayed until 1810, by which time the Quartel de Bexar or San Antonio Barracks were constructed, and the Alamo was again abandoned.

By the time Moses Austin arrived in 1820, much of the old Presidio de Bexar had been dismantled or incorporated into buildings surrounding the Military Plaza. The old commandant's quarters had been expanded and renovated to house the governor. Bexar itself was becoming cosmopolitan by frontier standards and there was less need for fortifications than for barracks. The Alamo had served as a prison for opponents of Spanish rule during the Mexican War of Independence, but now the newly independent Mexican government chose to quarter troops there. They would continue to use the Alamo as a barracks until they were expelled from San Antonio.

The Battle

Every Texas student has been over the political differences between the federal government of Mexico and its northern states that generated the Texas Revolution. It is enough to say that when conditions under the Santa Anna dictatorship became intolerable, the Texans joined the movement to return to constitutional rule. In October 1835, fighting broke out between Texans and federal troops in Gonzales, the federals withdrew, and the Texans began moving on San Antonio. There followed an impasse which lasted until early December.

Finally on December 5, 1835, the Texans attacked San Antonio in two columns. Spurred on by tough old Col. Ben Milam, they took over the strongly built de la Garza and Veramendi houses, then fought from house to house, pushing the federal garrison out of the city. Milam died in the fighting, but the Texans pushed on.

The federal commander, Gen. Martin Perfecto de Cos, ordered his forces to entrench in the Alamo, but was now plagued by desertions. Texans manning captured artillery hammered away at the walls. On the fifth day of the battle, Cos asked for terms and surrendered 1,100 officers and men. The federals were paroled on a pledge that they would never again take up arms against the Texans, and that they would support the Mexican Constitution of 1824. Cos took his men and headed toward the Rio Grande.

After the fall of San Antonio, many Texans scattered in various directions. But the commander, Col. James Neill believed the Mexicans would be back in force. So did Sam Houston, who understood the situation in Mexico.

Until now, the Texans had faced a largely convict army, made up of men who had joined to escape prison sentences. But throughout 1835, the Mexican president, Maj. Gen. Antonio Lopez de Santa Anna Perez y Lebrón had been building up the military. A professional soldier and a dynamic officer, Santa Anna now had a loyal, highly disciplined fighting force. It was these troops, some 6,000 in all, which would be sent in several waves to Texas. To keep the Texans mobile in the face of this threat, Houston sent James Bowie to San Antonio with orders to Neill to blow up the Alamo and withdraw.

Bowie had other ideas. Instead of evacuating the Alamo, he was determined to defend it. He used his Mexican connections in the city to obtain support which the garrison had not previously received. Green Jameson, a young attorney with a natural talent in military engineering, began working on fortifications.

Bowie had brought 30 volunteers to the Alamo. At the end of January, Travis arrived with 25 regulars. On February 11, an illness in the family forced Neill to turn command over to Travis and depart. But Travis was not popular and realized it. The following day, he agreed to an election, which placed Bowie in command.

Bowie may have had support, but he lacked physical stamina. Disease and alcohol had undermined him, and soon he and Travis arranged a joint command. As Bowie continued to weaken, Travis's position became undisputed. More and more, the men looked to him for leadership.

Meanwhile, Jameson had strengthened the walls, built parapets, and had constructed a thick pallisade with a ditch in the open area between the Low Barracks surrounding the gate and the old chapel. Almeron Dickenson managed to get 18 guns serviceable, ranging from 4-pounders to one large 18-pounder.

Travis and Bowie had received an unexpected boost on February 8, when the colorful frontiersman and ex-Congressman David Crockett arrived with 12 sharpshooters. More and more men began to come, until the garrison was up to about 150. Travis knew that a large detachment was at Goliad, 95 miles away. Since a planned expedition from Goliad to Matamoros had never gotten off the ground, he reasoned they would be more useful at the Alamo. On February 16, he sent an urgent request to the commander at Goliad, Col. James Fannin. The plea was ignored. The same day, Santa Anna crossed the Rio Grande near today's Eagle Pass. By Feb. 21, he was camped with an advance guard on the Medina River some 25 miles south of San Antonio.

Two days later, the local population got wind of the situation and began preparing to leave. Travis could not believe the federal forces had moved so fast, and sent Daniel Cloud to the tower of San Fernando Church to post a lookout. About 1 p.m., Cloud spotted what seemed to be cavalry on a distant hilltop, the sun glistening on their lances through a light drizzle. He sounded the alarm. Travis raced to the top and saw nothing. He sent Dr. John Sutherland and John W. Smith to the hilltop to check. Looking down at the other side, they saw row after row of federal cavalry. Sutherland's horse slipped, so Smith hauled Sutherland up behind him and riding double, they galloped back toward town. Seeing them coming, Cloud rang the church bell. The Texans began filing out toward the Alamo. The gates closed on 150 fighting men and about 25 noncombatants such as women and children, and slaves brought in as man-servants to the officers.

Inside, Travis began sending messages. About 3 p.m. Sutherland and Smith were sent to Gonzales for help. Another message went to Fannin in Goliad. As the couriers left, federal cavalry rode into the Military Plaza in San Antonio. Protected by the guns of the Alamo, Texans searched nearby huts and fields, and gathered up dried corn and about 30 head of cattle.

Travis's next message went to Santa Anna asking for terms. The reply was a demand for unconditional surrender. Santa Anna had a blood red flag flown from the tower of San Fernando Church, signifying no prisoners would be taken in the event of an assault. Unbeknownst to Travis, Bowie was attempting to negotiate on his own. The action brought the same rejection, and cost him prestige with the men. So sick he could no longer stand, Bowie took to his cot and left the responsibility with Travis.

The following morning, federal artillery began bombarding the Alamo. During a lull, Travis wrote his greatest letter, the one in which he told the world,

The Alamo as we know it today is the old chapel building where Texans made their last stand on March 6, 1836. The building was never completed as a church and was largely a ruin during the siege. The gabled facade and the two outer second floor windows were added by the United States Army, when it took the building over as a supply depot.

"I shall never surrender or retreat." About sunset, Capt. Albert Martin slipped out with the letter and headed toward Gonzales.

Meanwhile, the Sutherland-Smith mission to Gonzales got response. The town's militia left for San Antonio on February 27. Two days later, on Leap Year night, they eased through the enemy lines and arrived at the Alamo at 3 p.m. March 1. Travis had already sent yet a third letter. It was given to Capt. Juan Seguin, who bluffed his way past a federal patrol, which stopped him on the road to Gonzales.

By now, the enemy batteries had moved closer, and were hammering away at the walls from just beyond the range of Crockett's long rifles. The Alamo was weakened and gaps were beginning to appear.

Travis sent his last message on March 3. It was given to John W. Smith, who had led the Gonzales contingent back. Now Smith left the Alamo for the last time.

On the afternoon of March 4, Travis summoned the garrison and explained the situation. The position in the Alamo was doomed. The men had the option to surrender, to slip out and try to escape, or to fight and die defending the post. One man, Louis Rose, also called Moses Rose, decided to try his luck. He slipped over the wall, bluffed his way through the lines, and was gone.

At 10 p.m. March 5, the bombardment ended. Fatigue took over now. Had Santa Anna chosen to attack silently, he could have taken the Alamo with minimal resistance. The garrison was asleep. As it was, he divided his men into four assault columns, with a fifth held in reserve. Orders had been sent to commanders. The men ate and then rested until midnight, when they were awakened and readied. At 1 a.m., Sunday, March 6, the federal army began moving quietly toward the walls, carrying scaling ladders, picks, and spikes. Cavalry prowled the countryside to make sure no Texan escaped during the confusion of the assault. No one raised an alarm. The pickets sent out by Travis were probably caught and silently bayoneted. By 4 a.m., the vast columns were in position. They lay down and waited.

Suddenly, the stillness was broken by the shrill sound of bugles playing Deguello, the ancient Moorish call for blood. The sound stirred the drowsy Texans who heard the roar of thousands of voices in the night. Then the Mexicans were at the walls. Travis was one of the first to fall, a bullet in his head.

Two assaults were repulsed. Santa Anna threw in his reserves for another attempt. This time, two of the milling, confused columns converged on a third, and the sheer pressure of those behind forced the federal troops to the walls. They came to a redoubt built of earth and timber in a crumbled section of wall.

Gen. Juan Amador climbed to the top and waved his men on. In the next moment, they were inside the Alamo. The defenders began an orderly retreat to the Long Barracks in the old convent building. Those trapped on the walls turned their cannon into the plaza and raked the enemy with loads of scrap metal and chopped up horse shoes.

Inside the Long Barracks, the battle began anew. The floors had been ripped up, with trenches for the defenders and traps for the enemy. With fist, knife, and gunstock, men grappled and slashed at each other in the darkness and smoke. Bowie died on his cot, and his body was tossed about on bayonets. Crockett fell at Green Jameson's pallisade.

The last stand was in the old chapel. The federals turned the Alamo's 18-pounder inward and battered away at the walls. Infantry secured the doorway and poured inside. Maj. Robert Evans tried to fire the magazine, but was shot down before he could reach it.

By the time the sun was well up, it was all over. Five prisoners were taken. Despite Gen. Castrillon's efforts, Santa Anna had them bayoneted. Cavalry caught others outside the walls and made short work of them.

Among the noncombatant survivors were Almeron Dickenson's wife Susannah and their young daughter. Santa Anna sent them on their way, to spread warning of what would happen to others who resisted his rule. The bodies of the Alamo defenders were stacked in alternate layers with wood. Grease and oil were poured on, and the whole was ignited. For two days the pyres burned. Only one defender, Gregorio Esparza was given a decent burial, because his brother served with Santa Anna.

Santa Anna left a garrison in San Antonio, while he took the main force deeper into Texas to his well-known rout at San Jacinto. When word came back of his defeat, the Mexicans stripped the Alamo of everything movable, then blew apart the walls and most of the quarters. A contemporary drawing shows the ruins, with only the chapel, Long Barracks and Low Barracks standing. They, too, deteriorated.

Aftermath

During a Comanche scare in 1840, three companies of troops were temporarily moved into the Alamo. But by 1848, when Theodore Gentilz painted it, the Alamo was a weed-choked ruin. The property itself was subject to disputes between the Diocese of Texas and the City of San Antonio over ownership.

The Alamo in this 1861 drawing flies the Lone Star of Texas, shortly after secession when Gen. David Twiggs surrendered U.S. installations to state troops. (From Harper's Magazine, Author's Collection)

Both sides leased it to the U.S. Army after annexation, and while they fought it out in court, the Army moved in.

The United States government spent about $6,000 to improve the Alamo and make it suitable for storage. The walls were stabilized, two second floor windows were installed in the chapel front, the entire building was roofed over, and the facade was given the familiar gable it has today.

When Texas seceded from the Union in 1861, state authorities demanded that federal property, including the Alamo lease, be surrendered them. The U.S. commander of the Department of Texas, Gen. David Twiggs did so and has been castigated by historians ever since. Until Lincoln took office however, the U.S. government drifted about without a policy on secession, and though Twiggs had repeatedly asked Washington for instructions, he had been ignored. Hence, the decision to surrender. When Col. Robert E. Lee came through a few days later en route from Fort Mason to Washington (See Chapter 6), he found the Lone Star flag flying over the Alamo. The Con-

federates continued to use the Alamo as a depot until it was gutted by fire.

The U.S. Army returned after the War Between the States, and rebuilt the Alamo as a depot. It was so used until that function was removed to Fort Sam Houston.

Ultimately the state managed to secure title to the chapel. But the Long Barracks was altered, built over, and commercialized, serving at various times as a saloon and emporium. Finally, in the early years of this century, the Daughters of the Republic of Texas managed to galvanize the state into action. Led by Clara Driscoll, who donated $18,000 of her own funds and signed notes for substantially larger amounts, the DRT managed to get the Alamo designated as a permanent shrine to its heroes.

A portion of the Long Barracks walls and courtyard were rebuilt in the 1920s and 1930s, and the lower level of the building was completely reconstructed as a museum for the 1968 exposition. A combination museum-souvenir building was erected in 1936.

The Quartel de Bexar

Ruins of a wall and two rooms, located behind Four Seasons Convention Center on South Alamo Street, across from Hemisfair Plaza.

The Quartel de Bexar or San Antonio Barracks appears to have been constructed about 1810, after the Spanish governing council decided to relocate the administrative portions of San Antonio to La Villita. It was enclosed by a wall just over 300 feet long on the north and south sides, about 90 feet on the east, and 69 feet on the west. Inside were a guard room, magazine, supply room, quarters for enlisted personnel and officers and noncommissioned officers, stables, and a central parade area.

The history of the Quartel is sketchy, but it appears troops were recruited here in 1811 to overthrow Spanish rule, and again that year in a counterrevolution to restore it. The Quartel occupies very little space in the military correspondence of San Antonio in the years prior to the War of Independence, since most troops were either garrisoned in town or in the Alamo. An officer of the Engineers, Col. Jose Juan Sanchez Navarro, wrote of being fired on from a small fortress which appears to have been the Quar-

tel, during the battle of San Antonio in December 1835. After that, it began to figure regularly in dispatches from the city.

On January 6, 1836, Col. James Neill wrote the provisional government that he had "two distinct fortresses to garrison" in San Antonio. On January 18, Green Jameson wrote a letter to Houston, saying the Texas forces would be removed to the Alamo, since there were too few to garrison both forts. Travis also mentioned it in his dispatch from the Alamo on February 25.

The Quartel appears to have been pulled down as Travis prepared to retreat to the Alamo, since none of the Mexican officers in San Antonio mentioned it in their letters, diaries, or dispatches during the seige. The Alamo was more suited to Travis's plans, as it had been partially fortified by Cos and offered a clear field of fire. On the other hand, the view from the Quartel was obstructed by the houses of La Villita in the immediate vicinity.

The Presidio La Bahia

On the east side of U.S. 183, just south of the San Antonio River in Goliad.

The Presidio of Nuestra Senora de Loreto de la Bahia del Espiritu Santo de Zuniga is the best restored Spanish interior fortress north of Mexico. It is also the site of the other great massacre of the War of Independence, that of Col. James W. Fannin's command on Palm Sunday, 1836, and figured heavily in the filibustering era of the early 1800s.

The Fort's Beginnings

La Bahia was the result of Spanish paranoia over the vague and occasional French incursions into

Texas. Added to this was continual lobbying by Franciscan officials for missions to the coastal Indians. The viceroy saw the chance to solve both problems at the same time. Accordingly, he appointed the Marquis of San Miguel de Aguayo, a wealthy Coahuila landowner, to lead an expedition and secure the coast for Spanish rule.

When Aguayo reached the Rio Grande, he sent Capt. Domingo Ramon ahead to the Bay of Espiritu Santo, to take possession of the country surrounding La Salle's old Fort St. Louis. Ramon arrived and raised the Royal Standard of Spain on April 4, 1721. When Aguayo arrived, almost a year later, the Presidio of La Bahia was already a fact. Aguayo placed

Col. J. W. Fannin Jr. and others wounded in the Battle of Coleto Creek in 1836 were shot in the plaza of La Bahia.

The garrison's Indian troubles stemmed not so much from direct hostility as from being caught in the middle of tribal wars. In 1795, Comanches took over Espiritu Santo on the grounds that missionaries were aiding their enemies the Lipan Apaches. Troops were called out from La Bahia to run them off. Another time, Lipans visiting the fort tangled with Tawakonis who had called at the mission, and before it was over, several other tribes had gotten into it. To complicate matters, the presidio not only had to guard Espiritu Santo, but was also responsible for the new missions of Rosario to the west and Refugio. A town had also grown up around the fort. Called La Bahia, it would one day become Goliad.

Filibustering Attempts

With the revolt against Spanish rule in Mexico, most Royalist forces were pulled into the interior of the country, leaving the frontier garrisons sorely depleted. With minimal defenses and a disputed border with the United States in Louisiana, Texas became a prime target for filibusters who had various plans of their own. After the original insurgent leader, don Miguel Hidalgo y Costilla, was captured and executed, one of his aides, Bernardo Gutierrez de Lara, escaped to Louisiana. There Gutierrez fell in with Augustus Magee, a West Pointer who had been assigned to the U.S. forces in the neutral zone between Spanish and American territory. Together they would dominate events in Texas and in La Bahia in particular, in 1812 and 1813.

In the early weeks, things went well. Gutierrez prepared leaflets proclaiming the Republican Army of the North, while Magee drilled incoming volunteers. In August 1812, they took Nacogdoches without a shot, then moved into the interior of Texas. The target was Bexar, but deciding it was too heavily defended, Gutierrez and Magee turned toward La Bahia instead. With only 160 men to oppose the 800 or so filibusters, the Spanish garrison abandoned the presidio, and the Army of the North moved in without opposition.

Governor Manuel Salcedo was already en route to meet the filibusters. On learning they had taken La Bahia, he raced there, arriving on November 7, 1812. He set up his headquarters in the Espiritu Santo Mission, began a bombardment, and on November 14, tried to take the fort by storm. The Americans went out to meet him, but were driven back inside the walls. Once there, however, they were too secure for an outright assault. Royalist forces were deployed to

the fort under Ramon's command and founded a mission nearby. After he moved on, the new post was augmented by a detachment sent from Bexar.

After several years of inept military command, it became obvious the presidio and mission would not succeed among the coastal tribes, so in 1726, the troops and missionaries were ordered removed to the Mission Valley on the Guadalupe River. Although the mission and presidio remained on the Guadalupe for the next 26 years, the presidio continued to be known as La Bahia—the bay. The mission and fort enjoyed some success at the new site. An inspection in 1730 commented on the discipline and smart appearance of the troops. Even so, another move was in the offing, this one purely strategic.

In the 1740s, Jose de Escandon undertook the last major Spanish expansion, the conquest of the Seno Mexicano. This was the area between Tampico and the Nueces, including the Lower Rio Grande. As settlements were founded along the river, a new road was necessary to connect them with San Antonio and East Texas. Consequently, in 1749, La Bahia and its adjoining mission of Espiritu Santo made one final move, to a ford on the Lower San Antonio River. Here, the fort was built on a hill commanding the entire area around what would become Goliad. The mission was built across the river. The following year, an inspection showed a single long barracks, individual quarters for soldiers with families, and a church. These were picket construction and thatched. At his own expense, the commandant had built a stone house with several rooms to be used as a blockhouse if the need arose. Later, the entire post was reconstructed in stone.

surround the presidio and both sides settled down for a prolonged seige.

The monotony was broken by skirmishing from time to time. But as the winter dragged on, an uneasy truce developed between the two sides. Magee accepted a dinner invitation from Salcedo, and while there agreed to surrender the fort, provided the Americans could return home. On his return, however, his countrymen rejected the idea. Magee locked himself into his quarters, and an election among the men quickly replaced him with Col. Samuel Kemper.

A note from Salcedo reminding Magee of his promise to surrender was rejected. With that, the governor decided to end the matter and take the fort by storm. The assaulting force managed to make the walls before Kemper rallied his men and counterattacked. The Royalists were driven back across the river to Espiritu Santo. That night, Magee died in his quarters, apparently a suicide. He had deteriorated badly since his surrender proposal had been rejected, and appears to have been completely irrational by the time of the assault.

On Feb. 14, the Spaniards lifted the seige and headed back to Bexar. The Americans pursued the Royalists, finally catching up with them at Alazan where Salcedo surrendered. Gutierrez had the governor and his staff shot. While the procedure was normal for Mexico, it disgusted Kemper and the Americans. Aggravating the situation was Gutierrez's insistence that Texas remain part of Mexico, while the Americans planned to attach it to the United States. The alliance fell apart. Many returned to the United States. The Americans who stayed were slaughtered in the disasterous Battle of Medina. This battle had a profound effect on a young Royalist lieutenant, Antonio Lopez de Santa Anna, who thereafter developed a contempt for American military ability.

One survivor of the Gutierrez-Magee expedition, Col. Henry Perry, was not finished with filibustering attempts. With 50 men, he returned to La Bahia in 1817, and demanded surrender of the presidio. The surrender was refused and Perry attacked. But the authorities in Bexar had been aware of his movements, and as his men pressed against the walls of the

A gun platform shows La Bahia's true character as a fortress. It is the best restored Spanish interior fort in the United States.

presidio, they were attacked from behind by cavalry. Twelve prisoners were taken. The rest were killed or dispersed, including Perry, who committed suicide.

Even with these debacles, filibustering continued. In 1821, Dr. James Long gathered a band of adventurers and built a mud fort on Point Bolivar, opposite Galveston. Leaving his wife and baby with a small detachment, Long took the main body of his forces to La Bahia, where again the fort was captured without a shot. For three days, Long held the presidio without incident. But on the fourth day, 700 troops arrived from Bexar, setting up positions from the house tops in town, which gave them a clear field of fire. After a short fight, Long was tricked into surrendering, and he and his men were marched to Mexico City. In the interim, however, Spanish resistance in the interior had collapsed and an independent government had formed. Long was shot, but his men were soon allowed to return to New Orleans.

The death of Long ended the filibustering period for La Bahia. The fort was now relegated to routine frontier garrison duty, relieved by minor skirmishing between Mexican troops and Indians. One important event, hardly noticed at the time, was the birth of a son to a Mexican officer named Zaragoza, who lived in a two-room house just outside the walls. When Zaragoza was transferred back to Central Mexico, he took the boy, Ignacio, who grew up in the interior. La Bahia-born Ignacio Zaragoza would become the general who defeated the French in the Battle of Puebla on May 5, 1862, the Cinco de Mayo of Mexican history.

Revolution and Massacre

The town of La Bahia, by now called Goliad, did not so much join the anti-government movement of 1835, as it was forced into it by the federals themselves. That summer, the supreme commander in Texas, Gen. Martin Perfecto de Cos, appointed Col. Nicolas Candelle as commandant of all the troops. Arriving in Goliad as part of a reorganizational tour, he jailed the mayor, disarmed the populace, ordered a $5,000 military levy against the town, impressed men into service, and instituted quartering of soldiers in homes. The local population was now entirely alienated from the federal government.

The town simmered along with the rest of the state. On October 2, open conflict between Texans and federals broke out in Gonzales. A week later, Capt. George M. Collinsworth led a detachment from Victoria to capture La Bahia. After dark, a scouting party encountered Col. Ben Milam, who was making his way home after escaping from prison in Monterrey. Milam, who would later die in San Antonio, fell in with the company, and his presence gave an additional boost to the men.

The main force waded the river below town. Led by locals, the troops arrived at the fort at 11 p.m. The sentry was taken completely by surprise and only had time for one shot before the Texans cut him down. They broke down the commandant's door and took him prisoner. In a few minutes it was all over. The federal garrison, which had been reduced to 24 men a few days before the attack, listed one man dead and two wounded. The only Texas casualty was a man with a slight shoulder wound.

The victory provided $10,000 worth of military stores, 600 stands of arms, and several pieces of artillery, all left in La Bahia by Gen. Cos. Receiving word that federal troops planned to retake the fort, Collinsworth sent for reinforcements. The attack never materialized, but the Texas garrison was boosted by two companies.

Collinsworth was promoted to major and transferred to the army besieging San Antonio. The men elected Philip Dimmitt, a man of proven leadership. Under him, the men functioned as a unified command, something unusual for Texas in that period. Even so, Gen. Stephen F. Austin sent Collinsworth back to replace Dimmitt, on the grounds that the latter had behaved with unnecessary harshness toward the citizens of Goliad. The charges were groundless, and their source is obscure. The men drafted a set of resolutions which protested Dimmitt's removal, while carefully shielding Collinsworth's feelings. The resolutions were signed on November 21, 1835.

Dimmitt's men had one further statement to make. On December 20, they signed a declaration of independence from Mexico. A flag showing a severed right arm in bend holding a sword was made and run up over the fort. This is the flag generally flown at La Bahia today.

Even as Austin left the Army to enlist American support for the Texas cause, Dimmitt remained in command at La Bahia. Collinsworth appears to have made no effort to subordinate him. Dimmitt stayed until January 1836, when he was routinely relieved by Col. James W. Fannin Jr. When Fannin took command, the fate of the garrison was sealed. Although he died a hero, he was eminently unqualified to lead troops in a critical situation.

Fannin's first move was to strengthen the dilapidated presidio. Unlike the Alamo, La Bahia was designed and built as a fortress and required virtually no alteration. The actual work involved refurbishing what was already there, and pulling down surrounding houses to provide a clear field of fire. The Zaragoza house is thought to have been razed as part of the effort.

Work was underway when Santa Anna invested the Alamo, and was still incomplete when Travis's second appeal came. On February 25, Fannin abandoned La Bahia and took his command to help Travis. He got no farther than the river. First, a wagon broke down just beyond the town, requiring a reshuffling of oxen. Then Fannin realized he had forgotten to load provisions, even though he had some 300 men. He managed to get most of the troops across the river, where he camped for the night. He had moved less than a mile.

Fannin's officers were losing confidence in him. They demanded a council of war, where it was agreed to return to the presidio. Meanwhile, Gen. Jose Urrea's division had rushed up from Matamoros on a forced march and made short work of a Texas expeditionary force assembled in San Patricio. Fannin's own correspondence shows he was aware of the danger in his position. Yet for all that, and despite the fact that the Alamo had by now fallen, he sent 28 men under Capt. Amon B. King to rescue a citizen who had remained too long in Refugio. King stumbled on Urrea's troops and sent back for reinforcements. Fannin sent another 125 men under Col. William Ward.

On the night of February 13, Fannin received orders from Houston to blow up the presidio and retreat to the Guadalupe. His refusal has been blamed on everything from stupidity to jealousy. In this case, we look to Dr. Joseph Barnard, who was present when the order came, for an explanation.

"Far from Colonel Fannin wishing to disobey the order, I know from his own lips that he intended to conform to it as soon as the Georgia battalion [King and Ward] should return; and I had heard him before this express a wish that General Houston would come to take command of the troops. The alleged disobedience of Colonel Fannin to Houston's order is an undeserved censure on a gallant soldier; that he wrote back a refusal I *know* [Barnard's emphasis] to be false."

Barnard's account is disputed by others who point out the darker side of Fannin's nature. Even so, Barnard's version is in keeping with Fannin's subsequent actions, as well as certain quirks in his personality.

Several days passed with no word from Refugio. Meanwhile, Col. Albert Horton arrived with a detachment to cover the retreat Fannin was supposed to make. On March 17, Fannin learned that the men sent to Refugio had been captured. King's men had been shot, while Ward's command remained prisoners. A council of war convened and the officers voted to retreat to the Guadalupe the following morning. Just as the council broke up, scouts reported Urrea was nearing Goliad. On March 18, the sun rose on Mexican scouts looking the fort over. Horton's men chased them across the prairie until Fannin lost sight of both groups. When they reappeared, Horton was being pursued by a much larger force. Horton led his men to the old Espiritu Santo Mission, where they prepared to make a stand. A day for retreat had been lost.

The following morning, Fannin sent Horton to scout the crossing at the river. Finding it clear, the main body of troops left the presidio and began the retreat. La Bahia was abandoned.

Three days later, on March 22, the Texans were back—as Urrea's prisoners. Fannin had been caught on an open prairie near Coleto Creek, and had attempted to make a defense. He had fought the remainder of March 19th, and into the 20th, without cover or water. Finally, he had realized his position was hopeless and had asked for terms. He had understood his men would be treated as prisoners of war, and that officers and men would be paroled to the United States. Urrea's version is that the Texans surrendered unconditionally.

The Texans were herded into the old garrison chapel at La Bahia, where they barely had room to move. The heat was terrific and the air foul. They were offered no sanitary facilities, and were given

Although mistakenly called a mission because of the garrison chapel, the Presidio La Bahia in Goliad was built from the ground up by the Spaniards as a fortress. La Bahia was the center of filibustering from about 1812 to 1820, as well as a focal point in the War of Independence.

only water at widely spaced intervals. After several days, they were allowed some slices of raw beef. Gradually, their treatment improved and they were allowed out into the quadrangle and given larger rations. Since Urrea had no medical staff, the physicians were put to work treating the men on both sides who had been wounded at Coleto. This would later save those men's lives.

Meanwhile, messages had been shuffling back and forth between Urrea's headquarters in Victoria and Santa Anna in San Antonio. Evidence indicates Urrea was no butcher, and his bloody victories at San Patricio and Victoria had been enough. While he insisted Fannin had surrendered at discretion, he was quite willing to honor any understanding his prisoner may have had about parole.

But Urrea reckoned without Santa Anna. Orders came that the prisoners were to be shot. In an effort to stall, Urrea asked for clarification. Santa Anna lost patience. He repeated the order with several copies, each dispatched to Victoria by a different courier. Urrea had no further excuses.

The prisoners now not only included Fannin's immediate command, but Ward's, which had been returned from Refugio. There was also a fresh group from the United States, which had been captured immediately upon arrival at Copano. Many Texans had been wounded at Coleto, including Fannin himself, who was barely able to walk.

On Palm Sunday, March 27, the physicians were told to leave the fort and await further orders. Dr. Barnard struck up a conversation with an American-educated Mexican named Martinez. "At length," Barnard wrote, "we were startled by a volley of firearms, which appeared to be in the direction of the fort. [Dr. Jack] Shackleford inquired: 'What's that?' Martinez replied that it was some of the soldiers discharging their muskets for the purpose of cleaning them."

In reality it was firing squads. Shortly after the doctors left, the men had been marched out of the fort in three columns. They had been told they were heading for the coast to embark for the United States. A few hundred yards out, the guards called a halt and the killing began. The prisoners broke for the nearest brush in an effort to make the river. Some 28 managed to escape. The rest were hunted down and killed.

A Mexican colonel, sickened by the whole thing, told the physicians what was happening. Barnard recalled "the utmost distress" on the officer's face when he said, "These are not my orders, nor do I execute them." The gunfire continued. "The sound of every gun that rung in our ears told but too terribly the fate of our brave companions, while their cries, which occasionally reached us, heightened the horrors of the scene," Barnard wrote. It was particularly hard on Shackleford. His son was among those shot.

Then came the turn of the wounded. The crippled Fannin was ordered out into the quadrangle and dispatched with a shot in the head. Then, "the wounded lying in the hospitals were dragged into the fort and shot. Their bodies, with that of Colonel Fannin, were drawn out of the fort about a fourth of a mile and there thrown down."

Again, there was a funeral pyre. But unlike the pyre at the Alamo, the remains of Fannin and his men have definitely been identified. The monument near the presidio in Goliad is in fact a tomb.

Ruin and Restoration

After the War of Independence, the presidio lost importance. Goliad was moved across the river. The once-thriving town of La Bahia, which had more than 1,000 inhabitants before the war, dwindled to a scattered slum in the shadow of the old fort. By 1850, the entire presidio was in ruins except for the chapel, which was used as a residence by Judge Prior Lea. The Roman Catholic Church gained possession, and a few years later, Frederick Law Olmsted found one lone priest living to one side of the chapel, ministering to the needs of the people in what remained of the town. Gradually, the chapel itself deteriorated, although it continued in use as a church. Ultimately the structure was stabilized and restored. In 1946, the artist Antonio Garcia painted a fresco of the Annunciation of the Virgin on the rear wall.

In 1963, excavation and restoration of the entire presidio began under the sponsorship of the Diocese of Corpus Christi and the Kathryn O'Connor Foundation. Today, it has been rebuilt to appear as it did in the time of Fannin's occupancy. The commanding officer's quarters houses a museum, a cannon has been placed on the northwest bastion, and the sally port has been reconstructed, along with the guardroom and other structures. Just outside the walls, the Zaragoza House has been rebuilt and is a museum dedicated to Ignacio Zaragoza and the Intervention Period in Mexico. A cleared, landscaped area just off U.S. 183 leads to the Zaragoza statue donated by the people of Mexico.

Real Presidio de San Saba

On a county road leading to the golf course, just south of U.S. 190, about one mile west of Menard. Ruins are visible from 190.

The Presidio de San Luis de las Amarillas, later known as the Real Presidio San Saba, was the last major Colonial fort in the interior, and marked the farthest extent of Spanish dominion. Ill-advised and ill-fated from the start, it would always be associated with treachery and martyrdom.

The presidio and mission at San Saba came from over-zealous religion, the natural desire to defend the settlements, and the traditional Spanish weakness for chasing down unproven reports of mineral deposits. Since its founding, San Antonio de Bexar had been subject to raids by Apaches from the west. But even as they raided, the Lipan Apaches themselves began to feel pressure from Comanches. Simultaneously, rumors began drifting back to Bexar of vast silver deposits in Apacheria, deposits ultimately called the Lost Bowie Mine.

In their on-again-off-again wars with Spain, the Apaches had seen enough to know Spanish weaknesses. Consequently, an Indian delegation came to San Antonio to ask for a mission, something the Apaches knew would excite the extraordinarily powerful priesthood. Once the priests had become enthusiastic, it was simply a matter of waiting for authorization from Mexico City. Then, the priests and soldiers would come into Apacheria, and the Apaches could play Spaniard against Comanche.

The bureaucracy labored, approval was received, and in April 1757, Col. Diego Ortiz de Parilla set out for Apache lands on the San Saba, with garrison troops, settlers, and missionaries. A mission was built east of the river, and a presidio was built to the west. These were initially log buildings enclosed by wooden stockades. The settlement around the presidio may have had as many as 400 people.

Despite all the assurances in Bexar, the Apaches ignored the mission once it was established. As the months dragged on, none showed any particular interest in coming. However, some friendly Indians warned of an impending disaster. The entire frontier was put on alert, but as the new year came around and nothing happened, the Spaniards relaxed. Spring

A round tower protrudes from the corner of the old Spanish presidio of San Saba near Menard. Originally a wooden stockade, San Saba was rebuilt in stone following the 1758 massacre of the nearby mission. It was never a success.

brought tall grass. With it came the season of the Comanche moon. With plenty of grass for their horses and the full moon to light their way, the Comanches ranged far and wide.

The full moon came in mid-March. Every Lipan Apache disappeared. Then one morning, mounted Indians rode through the Spanish pastures and made off with 60 horses. This was enough for Col. Parilla. He called the garrison to general quarters and sent a message to the missionaries to come to the presidio. They refused, and after several days, Parilla rode over to the mission on March 15, to deliver the order in person. After some arguing, Alonso Giraldo de Terreros, father-president of the mission, agreed to move the following day. Parilla left a squad of soldiers and returned to the fort.

The next morning, March 16, the mission was shaken by the cries of 2,000 Comanches gathered outside the stockade, many armed with French weapons. The soldiers rushed to their stations and waited for the order to open fire. Terreros refused and allowed the Comanches to enter the fort. One of the few mission Indians slipped away to the presidio and gave the alarm. Parilla sent a squad of soldiers, which ran into a war party coming from the mission. In the ensuing battle, only one Spanish soldier managed to escape.

By now, the Comanches at the mission were busy looting it. When the war party returned with Spanish scalps, the slaughter began. Terreros was shot almost immediately. Fray Jose de Santiesteban was beheaded. The third priest, Fray Miguel de Molina managed to hide with one small group of Europeans in the chapel, while the killing raged around them. That night, they escaped to the presidio.

Three days later, when Parilla was sure the Comanches had left the area, he returned to the mission with Molina. The bodies were recovered and removed to the presidio for burial. The mission bell was also hung in the presidio, and tolled until sunset, March 19, as burial details finished with the bodies of the victims.

The attack on the San Saba mission threw the entire countryside into panic. Even San Antonio felt threatened. Appeals for help were sent to every garrison in Texas and Coahuila, but they, too, feared attack and refused to budge from their own forts.

Parilla proposed abandonment of the San Saba project, and proposed a mobile expedition against the Comanches. The abandonment was rejected, since it would mean surrendering the area to the enemy. However, the northern expedition was approved. In August 1759, Parilla left San Antonio with San Saba garrison troops and militia from as far away as San Luis Potosi and Queretaro. Moving north, he attacked and subdued a Tonkawa village. Parilla

pressed on until he reached a Taovayas village on the Red River on October 7. Here the Indians had established a stockade with breastworks, and were heavily armed with modern, French weapons. To cap it off, they flew the French flag. As the Spaniards surrounded the fort, more Indians closed in behind them, catching the Spanish in between.

After four hours of fighting, Parilla managed to cut his way out, abandoning the cannon behind him. He reached the San Saba Presidio after a bitter, 17-day march. Ever after, Spain would consider France directly responsible for the massacre of the San Saba Mission.

Parilla was replaced at San Saba by Capt. Felipe de Rábago. Arriving at the presidio in 1760, he undertook a major reconstruction. Work began in October 1760 on replacing the wooden stockade with a substantial stone fort, and took a little more than a year. This included a quadrangle with three small bastions on the corners, and a large, round tower on the northwest corner.

Rábago also resolved differences with the Lipans, and new missions were founded under San Saba's protection. Even so, the presidio itself was under continual threat from Comanches. In 1764, Rábago had to appeal to San Antonio and Coahuila for help. After a hard battle between Indians and San Saba troops on the Llano in 1766, he asked for an expedition to destroy the Taovayas fort once and for all. This request was deferred, pending the arrival of the Marquis de Rubí on an inspection tour. By early 1767, the situation had become so bad that Rábago removed the garrison's horse herd to Coahuila for safety.

A ruined arcade at San Saba.

When he arrived, Rubí saw San Saba's position was untenable, and agreed to recommend it be abandoned. That done, he continued his tour. But before the recommendations had filtered through the bureaucracy, the danger at San Saba had become critical. In June 1768, Rábago abandoned the presidio without orders.

Spain's failure to hold the San Saba changed the character of its rule in Texas. From then on, the Spaniards were on the defensive, holing up in presidios and rarely venturing beyond the settlements, except in force. The vast territory between San Antonio and the Rio Grande would remain in hostile hands for more than a century, until another nation settled the Indian question for good.

Empty now, the San Saba Presidio began the slow process of decay. During the next 100 years, occasional military expeditions would pass through, along with a few enterprising individuals. Among the latter was James Bowie, who visited in 1829, while searching for the legendary silver vein that came to be called the Lost Bowie Mine.

In 1847, Dr. Ferdinand Roemer, a German scholar camped in the ruins, and found the remains of the walls, bastion towers, round tower, and sally port, along with some of the main presidio structures. Dr. Roemer's description is very close to the ruins which exist today.

The fort was restored to some extent for the Texas Centennial in 1936, after which it was allowed to deteriorate again. Several years ago, some evidence of damage to the walls was found, along with tracks of a heavy machine. No one was charged with any offense, but legal authorities put certain individuals on notice. No damage appears to have occurred since then.

The Stone Fort

On the campus of Stephen F. Austin State University in Nacogdoches, about one block east of U.S. 59.

"Stone Fort" is a misnomer, which came to be applied to this particular structure sometime in the middle of the last century. Through much of its earlier history, it was referred to as the Stone House. In fact, it was a house. But at the same time, it was fortified, and served as a defensive position at least once during the civil strife which permeated East Texas prior to the War of Independence.

The Stone Fort owes its existence to a rare pioneering spirit among a group of Spaniards willing to disobey orders and strike out beyond the protection of the presidios. These people had been relocated in 1772, when Spain closed out its northeastern settlements. Some 500 self-reliant pioneers were moved to Central Texas, directly under Royal authority, in a climate and terrain they considered unbearable.

The settlers finally obtained permission to return to East Texas, where they founded the settlement of Bucareli, named for the reigning viceroy. But in 1778, Comanche raids made the site untenable. In defiance of government edicts, the community leader, Antonio Gil y Barbo led the group deep into the woods, to the site of the old Presidio of Nacogdoches. There, in April 1779, they founded a new community in familiar territory near their original homes. The government accepted it, and appointed Gil y Barbo as administrator.

Gil y Barbo set about making the town a trading center. He laid out streets and on the main thoroughfare, built the Stone Fort as a trading post. Because of his official position, it served as a public building as well.

In 1790, Gil y Barbo resigned under accusations of smuggling. He was arrested the following year, and although subsequently cleared, he was ordered not to return to Nacogdoches. It was ten years before he saw the Stone Fort again.

Although Gil y Barbo retained title to the Stone Fort, it had become so thoroughly identified with the government, that it was used as a land office, and by 1800 had become a military barracks as well. The following year, troops from the Stone Fort hunted down the filibuster Philip Nolan and imprisoned survivors of his expedition there for a month, before they were marched to the interior for trial.

Meanwhile, Gil y Barbo had returned to Nacogdoches. But in 1805, he had more legal troubles, and sold the building to Jose de la Vega, who in turn sold it to William Barr. Regardless of these transactions, soldiers still occupied the Stone Fort. And as trouble

The Stone Fort in Nacogdoches was built in 1779 by Antonio Gil y Barbo and served for many years as trading post, barracks, court, and civic center. It was dismantled in 1902, and most materials disintegrated due to neglect in storage. The present building has so little of the original materials that it is essentially a replica.

with American filibusters, boundary jumpers, and "lost" U.S. military expeditions continued, the Army showed no signs of leaving.

In 1810, Gov. Manual Salcedo went personally to Nacogdoches to settle old land claims. For six weeks during his stay, the Stone Fort served as seat of the Royal Government in Texas. Among those validating title was William Barr, who went into partnership with Samuel Davenport. As owners of the Stone Fort, they operated a mercantile business there, sharing the building with the soldiers.

The Gutierrez-Magee Expedition, which reached its peak at La Bahia, first gained ground at Nacogdoches. Gutierrez and Magee raised the green flag of their army over the Stone Fort and made it their headquarters. When they left for the interior, Rueben Ross was placed in command at Nacogdoches. Ross returned to the United States for reinforcements, and brought back a Philadelphia printer, who published Texas's first newspaper, *Gaceta de Tejas*, in the Stone Fort.

The collapse of the Gutierrez-Magee effort brought reprisals from the Royal forces. But the Spanish hold on East Texas was too shaky, and gave way to Dr. James Long. Again, the Stone Fort was used as a filibuster's headquarters, and a second newspaper, the *Mexican Advocate*, was published.

Independence from Spain brought Mexican officialdom to the building. With it came American empresarios, who obtained large tracts of land from the state government to parcel out as they saw fit. Haden Edwards became empresario of East Texas, and called on all property owners in the area to report to the Stone Fort and validate title or face forfeiture. Not many property owners remained after all the filibustering, but the action polarized old settlers—including many former Americans—against Edwards's newcomers. A suspicious election brought further troubles, until 1826, when the President of Mexico ordered Edwards's own grants forfeited. A group of citizens arrested Edwards and several others, and convened a court-martial in the Stone Fort. Although guilty verdicts were returned, no action followed.

Seeing his rule threatened, Edwards called together a group of supporters and malcontents, and declared the area to be the independent Republic of Fredonia. Government troops, including American militia under Stephen F. Austin, rushed toward Nacogdoches, and the Fredonia movement fell apart.

The Stone Fort was again garrisoned after the Fredonia Rebellion. In the spring of 1832, the local commandant, Jose de las Piedras, went to Anahuac to let William Barrett Travis and Patrick Jack out of jail and fire the Mexican officer who had imprisoned them. But while he was enroute, fighting broke out in Velasco. To avoid a confrontation when he returned to Nacogdoches, Piedras ordered all citizens to turn in their firearms.

This was too much for the East Texans. When they brought their guns to Nacogdoches, they came ready to fight. Piedras deployed his troops to the Stone Fort, the nearby Red House, and the church, and prepared a defense. The Texans worked their way behind the fort, then charged. They were beaten off and several of them were killed. Later in the day, Piedras ordered the Stone Fort vacated, and concentrated his forces in the Red House. After a failed attempt to slip out that night, he withdrew back to the Stone Fort, where he held out for one more day until he surrendered and evacuated the area.

Nacogdoches was far enough north to be removed from direct involvement in the War of Independence, so the Stone Fort was used more for civil functions than military. The building had again been sold, this time to Juan Mora and Vicente Cordova. Since they held the respective offices of district judge and district attorney, the Stone Fort served as a courtroom. It continued in this capacity under Primary Judge Adolphus Sterne and District Judge Robert (Three-Legged Willie) Williamson during the Republic.

Finally, after more changes of ownership, sometimes involving litigation, the house became the property of John S. and Harriett Roberts, who operated a saloon there. It was during this period that the name "Stone Fort" first came to be applied. The building remained a saloon until the end of the century.

In 1901, yet another set of owners announced the building would be demolished. This didn't set well with the Cum Concilio Club, made up of the city's leading ladies. An agreement was made to remove the house elsewhere for historic preservation. The place was dismantled in the summer of 1902, and the materials stored in a vacant lot, where they deteriorated rapidly. The "stone" was not in fact stone, but cakes of iron ore, which crumbled when disturbed. After the Stone Fort was reconstructed nearby, it bore no resemblance to the original building.

With the Texas Centennial in 1936, the Stone Fort was again dismantled and reconstructed, this time at its present location on the campus of Stephen F. Austin State University. By now, so little of the original material remained that the present building is a replica, albeit an accurate one. Even so, it is well worth the visit. Given its size and design, it has a remarkably well-planned and complete museum of the area, from Pre-Columbian times through the nineteenth century.

Fort Parker

A state park on Texas 14 between Mexia and Groesbeck.

Although the wooden stockade is a replica of the original log fort, Fort Parker was reconstructed using the basic pattern of upright log stockades of the early nineteenth century. The log homes of the settlers line the inside walls of the stockade and the stockade itself forms the back wall of the cabins.

The cabins are made of large cedar logs with mud chinking in between. In the summertime, the chinks were knocked out to let the breezes blow through the dwellings. The Indians had been peaceful for a long time, so the settlers had begun leaving the main gates open during the day, to allow more breeze to circulate.

The Fort Parker Massacre

The gates were open one hot day in 1836 when the Indians came. By the end of the day, the once busy fort was quiet. The screams of the wounded and dying were silent. There wasn't a sound except for the wind blowing through the compound.

Fort Parker was established in 1834, when the Reverend Mr. Daniel Parker brought his Predestinarian Baptist movement to Texas. Since Mexican law did not allow the organization of Protestant churches in Texas at that time, Parker organized his congregation in Illinois, then moved it down to a point near the Brazos where the settlement was established. Two years passed without incident. Some of the settlers moved outside the walls. Discipline was relaxed.

Most of the able-bodied men were in the fields a few miles from the fort on May 19, 1836. A band of Comanches, with a few Kiowas and Caddoes rode up to the gate under a flag of truce. When Benjamin Parker went out to parlay, they demanded beef. He refused and was promptly impaled on a lance. The Indians stormed into the fort. Elder John Parker was scalped, disemboweled, and emasculated before the Indians finished him. Ben and Silas Parker died, as did Sam and Robert Frost. Granny Parker was pinned to the ground with a lance and raped. She managed to survive. Several other women were raped as well, and two later died. By now, the Parker men were rushing in from the fields with rifles blazing. The Indians took off, carrying Rachel Plummer and her son James, Elizabeth Kellogg, and Silas Parker's children, six-year-old John and nine-year-old Cynthia Ann.

That night, the terrified survivors hid in the woods, leaving their fort alone in silence. After several weeks of hardship, they managed to make their way to civilization. Meanwhile, the Indians threw a victory celebration, part of which was the torture and gang rape of Mrs. Plummer and Mrs. Kellogg. Then the party split up, taking their captives in various directions. Mrs. Plummer lived as a Comanche slave for 18 months, until she was ransomed by a Comanchero. She died soon after her return to Texas. Mrs. Kellogg was taken by the Caddoes, who sold her to the Delawares. She lived with them until December 1836, when Gen. Sam Houston managed to buy her freedom. John Parker and James Plummer were ransomed in 1842. By then, John was thoroughly Indianized. Eventually he returned to the Comanches and went to live in Mexico.

The Search for Cynthia Ann

This left Cynthia Ann unaccounted for. She was seen several times over the years, particularly in the area around Fort Chadbourne. She never allowed whites to get really close to her, but the sightings were enough to send her uncle Isaac Parker searching. For almost 25 years, he chased down rumors, interviewed captured Indians, and met with ransomed whites. He checked newspapers and public records. Finally, in January 1861, he arrived at Camp Cooper, near what later became Fort Griffin, where a company of Sul Ross's Rangers had some Comanche prisoners. One of them was a white woman. By now, it was an old story to Isaac, but he went to look anyway.

When he arrived, it was obvious the woman had been with the Indians since childhood. She could not speak English and was being questioned through an interpreter.

"I told the interpreter if she was the daughter of Silas Parker, her name was Cynthia Ann," Isaac later recalled. "When she heard that, she slapped her breast and said, 'Cynthia Ann, Cynthia Ann.' Then the question was settled."

The story of Cynthia Ann Parker was one that was often seen during the Comanche Wars, but unique because of its outcome. Like John, she had quickly assimilated into the tribe. In her early teens, she had married the young chief Putak Nacona, with whom she had three children. The oldest was a boy, whose features and skin color were those of a Comanche. But he was extremely tall and had blue-grey eyes. His name was Quanah.

On December 18, 1860, Putak Nacona's band was camped along the Pease River when Sul Ross's Rangers attacked in the middle of a blowing norther. The Rangers took the prisoners to Camp Cooper, where Isaac Parker found Cynthia Ann. With her was her infant daughter, whom the Parkers named Prairie Flower.

For Cynthia Ann, the return to the Parkers was a tragic mistake. Although she had a grant of land and many blood relatives, she made several attempts to escape back to the Indians. Finally, she overcame her fear of the whites and got along reasonably well. Then Prairie Flower died, and Cynthia Ann lost all will to live. She held on until 1871, when she starved herself to death.

The compound at Fort Parker shows corral, blockhouse, cabins, and rifle stages along the walls. This was typical of the forts built by pioneer families in wooded areas, although not representative of U.S. Government posts, which were open. The present stockade was reconstructed on the original site.

Only the oldest son survived to adulthood. He took his mother's name and became Quanah Parker, last and greatest of the Comanche war chiefs. Although he fought the whites bitterly, Quanah was a realist, who knew the Indian ways were dying. After the Battle of Palo Duro Canyon in 1874 (see Chapter 4), he accepted surrender terms and led his band to the Fort Sill Reservation in Oklahoma. In 1886, he became a federal judge and spent his life improving Indian-White relations. In 1910, he had his mother's remains removed to Oklahoma. The following year, he died. They are buried together at Fort Sill.

Present-Day Fort Parker

Fort Parker is divided into two sections, a few miles from each other on Texas 14. Fort Parker State Park is purely recreational, with camping and outdoor facilities. The reconstructed stockade is at Old Fort Parker. It was rebuilt on the original site in 1936, after careful study. A blockhouse is built by the main gate, and a second one is on the opposite corner by a little opening called the spring gate. The latter leads to a nearby spring where the settlers got their water. It was through the spring gate that several escaped the massacre of 1836.

By following a park ranger's directions, you can drive to the well-kept Fort Parker Cemetery, established in 1836 as a burial ground for the massacre victims. There are graves from that date right up to the present day. It is a quiet spot, and perhaps has some of the peace Preacher Daniel Parker sought for his people. In the center is a monument topped by statues of a pioneer family. Down each shaft are the names of the families in the fort, those killed and wounded, and some of those captured.

II
THE RIVER FORTS

When Texas entered the Union, the federal government's first concern was not Indians but Mexicans. Mexico had served notice that U.S. annexation of Texas would be regarded as an unfriendly act. And although the Republic of Texas—and the United States—claimed the Rio Grande as the southern boundary, the area north of the Rio Grande to the Nueces River was legally part of the State of Tamaulipas. So when Gen. Zachary Taylor moved his troops to a campsite opposite Matamoros on the Rio Grande, war became inevitable.

Even after the Mexican War when the border was secured, a string of forts along the Rio Grande seemed advisable, for three reasons. American rule had brought commerce and development to the area, particularly after gold was discovered in California.

Argonauts could cut their travel time by taking a ship to Point Isabel on the Texas coast, then going upriver under the guns of the military until they reached a convenient staging point. From there, they could strike out across the desert to California. There was also the problem of local bandits, who frequently made forays across the border from Mexico. And finally, Apaches and Comanches wandered along the river looking for trouble.

Except for the earthworks at Fort Brown and Camp Crawford (Fort McIntosh), these posts were open cantonments, with the principal structures built around a parade ground. Construction was largely masonry, and for that reason, as well as the fact that they were used for almost 100 years, the remains of these oldest of federal forts in Texas are also among the best preserved.

Fort Brown

Extending southeast from International Boulevard, by Gateway International Bridge in Brownsville.

If a military installation could have a gender, Fort Brown would be the grande dame of all Texas forts. Established in 1846, it remained in use in some form or another for almost a century, until it was finally abandoned. With the possible exception of Fort Bliss, it has the longest service record of any Texas post.

The Mexican War

Fort Brown had its beginnings in the spring of 1846, when Gen. Zachary Taylor set up camp opposite Matamoros, some 35 miles inland from his supply depot at Point Isabel. Describing the founding of the post, correspondent T. B. Thorpe wrote that on April 5, 1846, "a small work, intended for the reception of the eighteen-pounders daily expected from Point Isabel, was thrown up opposite our camp." This "small work" was in fact a vast fortification, capable of enclosing five regiments.

In Matamoros, Gen. Pedro de Ampudia issued a protest, began strengthening his line of river fortifications, and threw up temporary bastions opposite the U.S. fort. On April 25, a detachment of dragoons under Capt. Seth Thornton was attacked north of the

river, several Americans were killed, and the rest were captured. When word of this reached Washington, President James K. Polk asked Congress for a declaration of war.

Meanwhile, Taylor worried about a possible Mexican advance on his supply base at Point Isabel. Consequently, he removed most of his troops there, leaving the nearly completed fortifications with 500 men of the Seventh Infantry and two companies of artillery, under command of Maj. Jacob Brown. If he was attacked, Brown was to signal by firing 18-pounders at regular intervals.

On May 3, Mexican artillery opened fire on the fort. For the first two days, the garrison endured the shelling. Bomb shelters protected the men from the antiquated Mexican shells, but time was running out. Mexican troops were being ferried across the river and lined up for an assault. Brown's own ammunition was growing scarce as he returned the enemy fire. On May 6, he ordered the 18-pounders to begin firing the distress signal.

As time passed, Mexican gunnery improved, and the walls started to show damage. Several horses were killed. At 10 a.m. May 6, Brown made an inspection tour. A shell screamed in and nearly severed his right leg. Doctors completed the amputation, and Brown was put to bed in one of the shelters.

Meanwhile, in Matamoros, Gen. Ampudia had been replaced by Gen. Mariano Arista, a veteran of the Texas campaigns and an aggressive fighter. On the night of May 7, Arista ordered an assault. But Mexican morale was low, and the troops wouldn't move. Frustrated, he continued the bombardment into May 8. That night, Brown died. Coincidentally, the Mexican guns fell silent.

The following morning, the garrison at the fort heard artillery in the direction of Point Isabel, signifying that the main armies had met. The firing resumed on May 10, and about 5 p.m., troops in the fort saw the first masses of routed Mexican soldiers fleeing across the river. Taylor had defeated Arista, first at Palo Alto and then at Resaca de la Palma. On May 18, U.S. forces occupied Matamoros, and the main theater of operations began to shift upriver and toward the interior. The garrison at the post now named Fort Brown was left in peace.

Bandit Wars

With the end of the war, Brownsville grew up around the fort as a village of merchants and soldiers. Steamboats brought goods in from Point Isabel, and took them on up to Rio Grande City, Roma, and Mier.

Visiting the post on a government inspection in July 1853, Bvt. Lt. Col. W. G. Freeman noted, "The present post does not occupy the site of old Fort Brown [the earthworks], but is above it. It had no defenses and the command are quartered in frame houses . . . Being the principal point on the river, a garrison must always be maintained here as long as the opposite bank is Mexican soil. Some arrangement for defense should therefore be made and barracks provided for at least a regiment of men. The present force is entirely inadequate."

Freeman also worried about health problems, as did inspectors who followed him over the next several decades. The post had periodic epidemics of yellow fever, cholera, and dengue, all associated with its semi-tropical location.

On the other hand, Col. Robert E. Lee, visiting the post in 1857 for court-martial duty, was struck by the tropical birds and plants around the post. Lee returned to Virginia later that year, to help settle his father-in-law's estate. During his absence, Fort Brown was deactivated and its troops dispatched to put down an Indian disturbance. The lack of military protection provided the opportunity for a local bravo

named Juan Nepumoceno Cortina to settle various scores.

Cortina has been described variously as an outlaw or a Robin Hood, depending on one's language and point of view. But recent research downplays his efforts to avenge grievances of the downtrodden Mexicans against American oppressors. Instead, the Cortina War appears to have been more of a gangster feud between various Mexican factions, in which the English-speaking population was largely in the way.

On September 28, 1859, Cortina led 100 men into Brownsville, and killed several persons on his death

An admiring citizen of Matamoros presented this highly decorated sword to Gen. Juan N. Cortina in 1864. By then the former outlaw chief had become a champion of the Republican cause in Mexico, and by extension, the Union cause in the United States.

list. He also tried to break open the Fort Brown magazine, where 128 barrels of powder had been left, but couldn't force the door. Mexican troops crossed over from Matamoros to calm things down, while citizens of Brownsville screamed for military protection. Their own hastily organized militia, the Brownsville Tigers, teamed up with Mexican militia and were soundly defeated when they attempted to chase Cortina into the countryside. Among other things, they lost two pieces of artillery.

The federal government regarrisoned Fort Brown, and Texas sent its Rangers. Lee also returned in 1860, this time as acting commander of the Department of Texas. Meanwhile, Maj. S. P. Heintzelman defeated Cortina at La Ebronal on December 14, 1859.

On May 7, 1860, Lee noted in his diary, "Have been engaged in corresponding with Mexican authorities; succeeded in getting them to issue orders for the arrest of Cortinas [sic]. . . . He has left the frontier and withdrawn to the Ceritos [sic] with his property, horses, etc."

The War Between the States

U.S. troops abandoned Fort Brown when Texas left the Union. Because Brownsville was an important blockade port, the Confederates garrisoned the post. After the French Intervention in Mexico in 1862, the U.S. government was faced with the possibility of direct assistance to the Confederacy. Consequently, 6,000 Federal troops were sent to Point Isabel, where they landed unopposed in the first week of November 1863.

At Fort Brown, Gen. Hamilton Bee realized his position was hopeless. On November 3, he ordered the post evacuated and burned, along with cotton stores in the government warehouse. Flames reached the magazine and exploding powder leveled most of the surrounding area. Advance units of U.S. troops reached the city the following day, with the main body arriving November 12.

Federal troops camped a short way upriver from the ruined fort. As there were still loyalists in Texas, the U.S. government had already organized the 1st Texas Cavalry. During the stay in Brownsville, the 2nd Texas Cavalry was also organized, and sent to New Orleans to serve the Union cause. The 1st Texas remained in South Texas, where on June 25, 1864, it was defeated by Confederates under Col. John S. (Rip) Ford at Las Rucias, upriver from Brownsville. Union forces evacuated the city, and on July 30, it was the Confederate turn to enter unopposed.

The rest of the war was a waiting game, with the Union Army at Brazos Santiago, opposite Point Isabel, and the Confederates in Brownsville. Finally, in May 1865, U.S. troops moved against the city. Ford engaged them at Palmitto Hill on May 13, driving them back but failing to break their lines. The waiting game continued a few more weeks until word arrived that the war was over.

Peacetime and Civil Strife

Occupation forces under Lt. Gen. Philip H. Sheridan arrived in Brownsville in June to reestablish federal authority and show support for the Juarez Government in Mexico. But no real effort was made to reconstruct the post until 1867, when renewed bandit activity forced a major concentration of troops. Fort Brown was rebuilt in brick, and these buildings make up a large portion of what remains today.

However, disease reappeared, with yellow fever epidemics reported in 1867 and again in 1882. A step in identifying the cause came when Maj. William C. Gorgas performed autopsies at Fort Brown in 1882. He eventually traced the cause to a mosquito, and this led to the ultimate conquest of the disease.

Life at the post was routine as the new century dawned. Soldiers came and went until the spring of 1906, when the First Battalion, 25th Infantry (Colored) was ordered to replace the white 26th Infantry. The 25th had a distinguished combat record in the Indian Wars, the Spanish-American War, and the Philippine Mutiny. Most of its men were career regulars, and discipline was generally excellent. But this was lost on local residents, who resented the idea of black troops.

Companies B, C, and D, consisting of 170 black soldiers and noncommissioned officers and five white officers, arrived in Brownsville on June 25. The local community closed ranks and incidents began. Tension mounted until August 13, when Mayor Frederick J. Combe conferred with Maj. Charles W. Penrose, the commanding officer, who ordered an 8 p.m. curfew at Fort Brown.

About midnight, shooting broke out beyond the low wall which separated the fort from the town. Thinking the post was under attack, the troops turned out with weapons and prepared a defense. Meanwhile, someone—it was never established who—stormed through the lower part of Brownsville, shooting the place up. Police Lt. Joe Dominguez's horse was shot, pinning him down and breaking his arm. Bartender Frank Natus was killed in the Ruby Saloon.

Not one shred of evidence ever connected the soldiers with the incident. Even the military .30-06 shell casings found at the scene had all the earmarks of a plant. Tests under similar lighting conditions, held at Fort McIntosh, determined it would have been impossible even to see the raiders, much less identify them as soldiers. Nevertheless on November 5, President Theodore Roosevelt signed an order dismissing all three companies from the service. While the officers were later exonerated by court-martial, none of the troopers or noncoms was ever tried.

With that, Fort Brown was again closed. So it remained until revolution in Mexico brought a new wave of violence, and the 16th Cavalry was sent to reactivate the post. Skirmishes were numerous during this period, and once a train was blown up. But by and large, the 16th patrolled and maintained a military presence in coordination with various National Guard units, while the bulk of the fighting went on between various revolutionary factions in Mexico.

Modern History

The 12th Cavalry took over Fort Brown in 1919, and remained until February 1941, when the various regular regiments scattered along the border were called to Fort Bliss and consolidated into the 1st Cavalry Division. The previous month, the 124th Cavalry of the Texas National Guard had been sent to the lower river, with the Headquarters and First Squadron at Fort Brown, and Second Squadron at Fort Ringgold. The 124th remained until May 1944, when it was transferred to Fort Riley, Kansas, in the first leg of its road to glory in Burma.

The following year, as Fort Brown neared the century mark, it was certified to the War Assets Administration for disposal. On July 22, 1948, the front 162 acres were turned over to the Brownsville School District for use as a junior college. Since then, the City of Brownsville and Texas Southmost College have gradually acquired rights to most of the post.

In 1973 Fort Brown again drew national attention, when the two surviving troopers of the ill-fated First Battalion, 25th Infantry were given honorable discharges. The government had at last corrected its old injustice against the black soldiers.

Today Fort Brown has been so extensively altered that you have to look for its buildings. A civic center, parking lot, library, and student center stand on the parade ground. The post hospital and its support buildings still stand, as do portions of officers row. If you look hard enough, you can find the commissary, post laundry, hay barns, granary, and noncoms' houses. The cavalry barracks were recently restored to their original external appearance.

One corner of the old Taylor earthworks from 1846 still exists by the golf course. An upturned cannon barrel imbedded in concrete marks the spot where Maj. Jacob Brown fell. This oldest portion of the post is being restored as a historic park.

The post hospital today serves as the administrative building of Texas Southmost College. With the exception of the two-story annex (far left) its exterior is little changed from when it was built.

The Casa Mata

On S. Degollado Street at its intersection with Republica de Guatemala Street in Matamoros.

If one is to include Fort Brown, common sense dictates mention of its Mexican counterpart, the Casa Mata. This is what the Mexicans call a "fortin," comparable to the American blockhouse.

The Casa Mata was built about 1840, and is the last vestige of the once-vast fortifications which enclosed Matamoros on the landward side. It was used during most of the nineteenth century in the various Mexican internal and external struggles. As late as 1913, the Revolutionary Gen. Lucio Blanco ordered some of the defenders of Matamoros executed on the Casa Mata grounds, after he captured the city.

The building underwent restoration from 1965 to 1970. The original walls and roof were stabilized, additions were constructed, and the grounds were landscaped. Today, it serves as a regional museum from the Pre-Columbian era to the present.

Fort Ringgold

On U.S. 83 in Rio Grande City, between Pete Diaz Jr. Avenue and the "Y" intersection with East Main Street.

Like King Tutankhamun, Fort Ringgold is significant by what is preserved, rather than what was accomplished. It is unique among Texas posts in that the original fort, built prior to the War Between the States, remains largely intact just behind the later one. With minimal alteration, it would serve very well as a movie set.

Fort Ringgold does not have an outstanding history. No great expeditions were mounted there against the Indians. It had one major action during the Cortina War and some skirmishing during the War Between the States. Beyond that, it was simply a solid duty post, largely subordinate to and overshadowed by Fort Brown or Fort McIntosh.

Antebellum Activity and the Cortina Wars

The post was established as Camp Ringgold on October 26, 1848, by Companies C and G of the 1st Infantry, under Capt. J. H. LaMotte. It was named for Bvt. Maj. Samuel Ringgold, 4th Artillery, who died at Palo Alto, and was built for its advantages in observing Mexican troops at Camargo, across the river and about five miles inland.

Nearby Rio Grande City—then called Davis Landing—was a steamboat port and offered convenient transportation.

Arriving at Ringgold in 1851, Teresa Viele, wife of an officer stationed there, wrote that it "rose before us on a high sandy bluff, its rows of long, low, whitewashed modern buildings, placed at regular intervals around a level drill ground, in the centre of which rose the flag-staff, with its colors hanging droopingly, unstirred by the sultry air. These buildings were the government store-houses, soldiers' barracks, and officers' quarters . . . There were no signs of vegetation around; not even a blade of grass was to be seen. The sentinels monotonously walking guard gave unmistakeable token of a military post."

Although the Ringgold garrison never appears to have had any direct problem with Indians, the threat did exist. Mrs. Viele's steamer was fired on by "Camaches" while heading upriver from Fort Brown. She

A current view of the barracks (left) and guardhouse (right background) of Fort Ringgold, shows efforts in preserving the post intact. The two-story barracks had mess halls, offices, and guardrooms on the ground floors, and sleeping quarters upstairs. The post is now used by the Rio Grande City School District.

also noted outings were limited to the immediate neighborhood of the post, and Indians occasionally wandered in to trade and talk horses.

Filibustering seemed to have been the major excitement during the Viele family's tour at Fort Ringgold. At this time, Gen. Jose Maria Carvajal was attempting to form a separatist government, and U.S. troops deserted to join him. The effort reached its climax when the filibusters engaged Mexican troops in Camargo and the sound of gunfire could be heard by the troops and families at Ringgold.

Robert E. Lee's court-martial duties brought him to the post on September 28, 1856, and he remained until court adjourned to Fort Brown on October 30. The old commanding officer's quarters was represented as the "Lee House" for many years, although evidence seems to indicate he used a tent.

In March 1859 Fort Ringgold was abandoned, as were Fort Brown and Fort McIntosh. But the outbreak of the Cortina War forced reactivation later in the year. On December 14, Maj. Samuel Heintzelman left Fort Brown with 165 U.S. regulars and 120 Rangers under Capt. W. G. Tobin. The same day, following the fight at La Ebronal, they were overtaken by another 53 Rangers under Maj. John S. Ford, and to-

gether the combined forces headed upriver. On the night of December 26 they caught Cortina at Rio Grande City.

The force attacked the following morning. Tobin struck Cortina's left wing, while Ford charged through the center to clear the way for the regulars. Cortina returned fire with two artillery pieces he had seized from the Brownsville Tigers (see "Fort Brown"). Hand-to-hand fighting developed until the regulars arrived, at which point the Cortinistas withdrew, leaving most of their provisions. They did take the two cannon, although the guns were abandoned on the road to Roma. The chase went on for about ten miles, until a Captain Stoneman dismounted his company of soldiers and forced one group of Cortinistas into the river. The rest dispersed.

As volunteers, the Rangers had the right to elect their own officers. Now that the fighting was over, they settled down at Ringgold to choose them. Tobin won over Ford by six votes. Ford then left for Brownsville, after which discipline fell apart among Tobin's men. One local resident claimed Cortina had stolen $200 worth of his property, and the Rangers had destroyed $1,000 worth. Tobin was ordered to Fort Brown for discharge on January 12, and the command was reorganized.

The Civil War

The War Between the States divided the Spanish-speaking citizens, just as it did those who spoke English. In April 1862 Capt. Refugio Benavides organized a company of soldiers for the Confederacy at Ringgold. With the exception of one lieutenant, every man was a Mexican-Texan.

Yet at the same time, the U.S. Consul in Matamoros was suspected of organizing others to raid into Texas. In December 1862 a wagon train escorted by five soldiers from Fort Brown was attacked by a group of Mexicans suspected of being in Federal service. One teamster escaped to Fort Ringgold, and a company of troops was dispatched to a local ranch. Some of the property was found there, and the huts of the Mexican-Texans who lived on the ranch were burned in retaliation.

Ringgold escaped the destruction that fell on Fort Brown when the Confederates evacuated it. In late 1863 Col. E. J. Davis marched in with two regiments of Texas Cavalry from the U.S. Army. With the Confederates gone from the area, Davis left a detachment of the Mexican-Texan 2nd Texas Cavalry at Roma and withdrew to Brownsville. The idea was to gather enough troops on the lower river to seize the Rio Grande as far as Fort Duncan, then march north and link with Federal troops who would push across from New Mexico. However, the plan never materialized, and the Confederates began building up for their own march to the sea.

The movement began when Col. Santos Benavides, Refugio's brother and the highest-ranking Mexican-Texan in the Confederate armed forces, rose from his sickbed to repulse a Union attack on Laredo on March 19, 1864 (See "Fort McIntosh"). Shortly thereafter, a unit under Col. John Ford, the former Ranger arrived, having fought its way down from San Antonio against Union irregulars. With Santos Benavides still sick, Refugio took command of the entire regiment, and joined up with Ford for the march downriver. The column arrived at Ringgold on May 2, and set up a base from which Ford planned his push to Brownsville. He advanced as far as Las Rucias, but outran his supplies and had to retreat back to Ringgold. Again, he marched downriver, entering Brownsville unopposed on July 30. After that Ringgold's role in the war was over.

Reconstruction

The garrison then settled down to boredom, and disputes among themselves and with the area's civilian populace. During this lull there was one near-riot and several murders.

American troops arrived in the summer of 1865, to reestablish federal authority and to keep an eye on French troops now occupying Mexico. In 1867, a three-year reconstruction began, in which the post assumed the general appearance it has today. Shortly after the renovation, the new facilities at Ringgold were described in a survey of the Military Division of the Missouri as consisting of "Quarters for four companies, with out-buildings, new, built of brick and well constructed; officers' quarters, nine sets, new brick buildings; hospital, new, built of brick; guardhouse; storehouses, two; baker, stable and corral."

As for the military land on which the post was located, the survey says, "No reservation has been declared. One thousand yards square occupied. Ten thousand dollars has been appropriated by Act of Congress for purchase of the site." The reservation was purchased and declared, and the post, which up until now had been Ringgold Barracks, received the permanent designation of "fort."

By now, however, Fort Ringgold had no purpose, other than to serve as a base for general patrol duties along the border. Aside from the border disturbances of 1915–16, there was minimal activity. The Second Squadron of the 12th Cavalry was assigned to Fort Ringgold, while the First went to regimental headquarters at Fort Brown. With the rifle area limited at Brown, the First Squadron would make a five-day hike to Ringgold every year, for two weeks of intensified firing-range training known as "rifle season."

Most soldiers left when the 12th Cavalry was ordered to Fort Bliss in 1940. On March 1, 1941, Fort Ringgold listed 400 men officially on active duty. The post was declared surplus and inactivated in 1944.

Ringgold has escaped the destruction visited on other forts as "progress" catches up with them. You can still drive past an old guard post and out onto the 1867 quadrangle, with barracks on one side, officers row on the other, and the hospital and administrative buildings on opposing ends. Behind officers row is the Antebellum post.

The main enemy now is decay. The post is used by the Rio Grande City School District for classes and support services. Prior to his retirement, then-School Superintendent S. P. Cowan discussed the status of the post, saying, "School taxes are levied and collected for school purposes. This hamstrings us as far as spending any money on it, except as a teaching aid for historical subjects. However, we spend what we can on maintenance as school property and try to get along." Even so, the deterioration has been noticeable within the last 10 years.

Fort McIntosh

On the west end of Washington Street in Laredo. Take the Washington exit on I-35 and follow it the entire length. The post is now Laredo Junior College, just over the viaduct which crosses the railroad yards.

Establishment and Construction

Fort McIntosh was established near the old Spanish town of Laredo on March 3, 1849. The post was originally founded as Camp Crawford by Second Lt. E. L. Viele, whose wife Teresa left such a thorough account of life at the river forts (See "Fort Ringgold"). In January 1850, the name was changed to Fort McIntosh, after Bvt. Col. James S. McIntosh, who was mortally wounded at Molino del Rey in 1847.

The post was slow in building. For a long time men lived in tents. By the time of the Freeman inspection of 1853 (See "Fort Brown"), the garrison had been moved into quarters originally constructed as kitchens, and which the report called "insufficient for the purpose to which they are now applied."

Yet in spite of this, the government took no action to alleviate the situation. In fact, no permanent barracks would be built for more than 30 years. This does not mean that the War Department was unaware of the problem. In 1856, when Col. J. K. F. Mansfield inspected the post, he still found troops living in tents and suffering from heat in the summer and cold in the winter. Soldiers got some shade by constructing awnings using posts which they had purchased with company funds, and the officers were putting up a building at their own expense.

Meanwhile, the men were wasting time and energy putting up an earthwork fortification similar to that at Fort Brown. Mansfield blasted the idea in his report, saying, "I do not consider this small field fort of any material strength or importance. The same labour would have put the men in comfortable quarters."

When they were not moving dirt, the troops patrolled against Indians and outlaws from Mexico. Mansfield wrote that soldiers from Fort McIntosh periodically chased down Indians on the Texas side of the river, at the request of the governor of Tamaulipas. Teresa Viele told of one particular expedition against Comanches, which got off to a bad start when the officer in charge found the men had been sipping whiskey from their canteens and were half-drunk before they got well into the march. He ordered the canteens emptied and punished one insubordinate trooper by dragging him some distance behind a horse.

The following morning, the soldiers sighted an Indian camp and charged into it. The surprised Indians scattered into the brush and were lost, although the troops managed to take control of the camp. Meanwhile, these Indians had joined up with a stronger band of Comanches, and ran across a second patrol from Fort McIntosh. There was a brief, vicious fight. At one point, the lieutenant in charge was about to shoot one hostile, when he saw it was an old woman pleading for mercy. He lowered his revolver and she lanced him to death. The sergeant took over, and the badly mauled troops managed to hold the field. Eight hostiles were killed, including the old woman. The first patrol, now sober, came onto the scene as these troops were dressing their wounds and tallying the dead.

Scouting intensified in 1858, and hostiles withdrew from the area. In February 1859, after a year without Indian encounters and with relatively cordial relations between U.S. and Mexican authorities, the Army ordered Fort McIntosh abandoned. However, it was reoccupied in February 1860, in response to the Cortina threat (See "Fort Brown").

The Confederate Occupation

Fort McIntosh was abandoned a second time on March 12, 1861, after the Texas forts were surrendered to state authorities. With no Federal troops, the occasional raids from Mexico were stepped up. Rumors flew that Cortina was massing strength at Guerrero for an incursion into Texas, and Santos Benavides took troops down from Laredo to stop him. On May 19, Cortina crossed the river just below

Soldiers at Fort McIntosh suffered in tents and makeshift quarters for over 30 years before a miserly Congress appropriated sufficient funds for real barracks, such as this one. When completed, they resembled barracks buildings found on nearly every major U.S. military installation from Texas to Hawaii. This structure, built in the 1880s, is the last surviving barracks building at Fort McIntosh.

Carrizo (Old Zapata). The following day, his scouts clashed with those sent out by Benavides. The Confederates had deployed at the fortified house of rancher Henry Redmond, and by May 21 Cortina had them surrounded.

A rider managed to get through the Cortina lines, and at dawn May 22 Refugio Benavides rode in with news that help was on the way. A relief column arrived later that morning. Santos Benavides took 40 volunteers for a direct attack, and caught Cortina with 70 followers just outside of town. The Cortinistas were driven to the river with 7 dead, 15 wounded, and 11 captured. As Benavides had no use for prisoners, his report hints vaguely that the 11 Cortinistas were executed on the spot.

For this battle, Santos and Refugio Benavides, and their uncle Basilio Benavides who had led the relief column, were cited in a general order. Gov. Edward Clark sent Santos an engraved pistol with a congratulatory letter.

But while Cortina was a dangerous nuisance, Benavides was largely concerned with Federal agents in Mexico, and possible efforts to disrupt the cotton traffic on the rivers. The main port of entry was at Eagle Pass (see Chapter 3, "Fort Duncan"), and there was a possibility of an attack there, as well as a Union thrust upriver from Brownsville.

For three years, Benavides remained continually in the field. In February 1864, he led his troops to Fort Duncan, to reinforce the garrison against a rumored attack. When it failed to materialize, he returned to Laredo, where he collapsed from exhaustion. Working from his sickbed, he arranged a shifting of the port of entry from Eagle Pass to Laredo, and made preparations to meet additional troops coming from San Antonio under Col. Ford.

Meanwhile, U.S. forces were not idle. On March 19 a Federal detachment of nearly 200 men from Brownsville arrived at the edge of Laredo, determined to seize the port. Benavides could only face them with 42 regulars and 30 militiamen. Getting up from his bed to prepare a defense, he sent a call for another 100 troops who were camped north of town. Then he gave orders that if the city fell, 5,000 bales of cotton stacked on San Agustin Plaza were to be burned, along with his own house. The streets leading into San Agustin Plaza were barricaded with cotton bales, and snipers were placed on the rooftops in case the Union troops broke into the city. Then he took the 42 regulars and set them out near Zacate Creek east of town.

The approaching Federals dismounted, formed into 40-man squads and advanced on the Confederate position. The Confederates allowed them to get within range and then opened up with careful, organized gunfire. Three attacks were repulsed, and the Federals were further disorganized by independent horse charges into their ranks. After three hours, both sides settled back into sniping at each other until nightfall.

Throughout most of the night, the people of Laredo expected another attack. Finally, at 2 a.m., the 100 men from the Confederate camp arrived in town. The following morning, a scouting party led by Refugio Benavides reported the Union troops had withdrawn. On May 22 a distant Confederate scouting party was mistaken for another Union advance, and Santos Benavides prepared to defend Laredo again. Too weak to stay in his saddle, he fell off and received a severe blow to his head. In a letter congratulating him for his defense, Ford worried about Benavides's health and urged him to turn command over to another ranking officer. Finally, Ford himself arrived to take command of the garrison at Laredo.

With Ford's arrival, the Confederates were strong enough to begin the downriver advance toward Brownsville. Laredo's role then receded into the backwater of the river war, until the final collapse of the Confederacy. In the summer of 1865 one company of the 62nd Infantry (Colored) arrived to reclaim Fort McIntosh on behalf of the United States, and reestablish Federal authority. A permanent garrison arrived on October 23 to find most of the buildings had been removed, leaving only the earthworks. Once again, troops camped in tents, while headquarters and the guardhouse were set up in the courthouse. Construction of a new post began in 1869.

Minor Skirmishes and Abandonment

During this period, troops had trouble with Kickapoos, who began raiding in the vicinity of Laredo in 1865. Patrols were stepped up, and while no major fights were reported, constant pressure on the Indians was maintained. In 1870, a scouting party from Fort McIntosh joined up with a unit from Fort Ringgold to push up toward Fort Inge at Uvalde. By the end of the year, the raids were tapering off.

But while the Indian problem faded away, internal troubles in Mexico spread across the river. Revolutionaries would strike in Mexico, then flee across the river into Texas before they could be captured. In April 1876 soldiers of fortune in Laredo fired across the river at Mexican troops in Nuevo Laredo, drawing return fire. A gun crew from Fort McIntosh was

sent into town. When Mexican troops fired at it, the crew began shelling Nuevo Laredo. The Mexicans ceased firing.

Ten years later, local politics boiled over, and troops were sent into Laredo to put down some of the bloodiest fighting in the area's history.

In the 1880s, the soldiers at Fort McIntosh finally got real barracks. These were two-story masonry, with wide verandas and balconies on either side. Construction continued until 1897, when the last major project was completed. After almost 50 years, Fort McIntosh finally assumed the appearance of a permanent military post. By now, though, it had been relegated to training duties and patrols, since there was no real need to maintain a garrison against a hostile enemy.

Fort McIntosh was used for experiments in military aviation in 1911 (see Chapter 3, "Fort Duncan"). Flying continued there until the 1930s, when the WPA built a low wall around the post, making take-offs and landings hazardous in military aircraft. However, in 1942 the Southern Liaison Patrol of the Civil Air Patrol was established in Laredo, and the old cavalry grounds at Fort McIntosh were found to be ideal for the light CAP planes. McIntosh was one of two bases used for patrol flights along the border from San Benito, Texas, to Douglas, Arizona, and in 18 months, more than 6,000 missions were flown.

Fort McIntosh was 97 years old in 1946, when orders came down for permanent abandonment. Bodies in the post cemetery were transferred to Fort Sam Houston, and preparations were made to terminate military affairs. On May 31 the flag was lowered for the last time, and the troops marched out and headed to the railroad station. The following year, the post was struck from the lists of military property and turned over to the City of Laredo.

Today, approximately half of the fort is intact. Laredo Junior College and Laredo State University use most of the buildings, and have erected modern structures on the parade ground. Three of the masonry barracks have been removed, although a fourth has been left standing. Most of officers' row is intact, as are the bakery, hospital, various company quarters, hay sheds, and granary. The oldest building on the post is the commissary, of uncertain date, which may have been a ranch house prior to the establishment of the post. It is now a gallery for the Laredo Art League. The Nuevo Santander Museum Complex has its main office, archives, and gallery in the old post chapel, and maintains a military museum in the guardhouse. By asking at the museum, one can obtain directions to the old earthworks, which are essentially intact, although not maintained as are those at Fort Brown.

Fort Bliss

A United States Army post comprising a reservation of approximately 1.25 million acres in Texas and New Mexico. The entrance generally used is off Airway Boulevard, north of Montana Avenue in El Paso.

The only true frontier fort still active in Texas today, and the largest air defense installation in the free world, Fort Bliss was moved four times before it was established on a permanent reservation. The post itself was founded in 1848. However, not until 1893 was the fifth and present site occupied.

Establishment

The original adobe post was set up on the Rio Grande to assert U.S. authority over newly acquired territory, and to defend against hostile Indians. However, in September 1851 troops were moved to Fort Fillmore, New Mexico, to remove them from what the departmental commander considered to be the corrupting influence of settlements. With the soldiers gone, Indian depredations stepped up, and within 2 years, 23 attacks had been reported. Consequently, an 1853 inspection report recommended reactivation. In January 1854, four companies of the 8th Infantry arrived and established a new post at Magoffin's Ranch, about a mile from the first site.

Up until now, the establishment had been called "Military Post Opposite El Paso, Texas." However, the Magoffin Ranch site was designated Fort Bliss, after Capt. William Bliss, Gen. Zachary Taylor's aide. Even after the post was activated, Indian raids continued, and no one could safely go out from it more than three miles without an escort. Troops from Fort Bliss worked throughout the 1850s to end this, and were active in most expeditions culminating with Gen. Benjamin Bonneville's Gila River Campaign of 1857.

The Civil War

When Texas left the Union, the post commander sent to Washington for permission to disobey Gen. David Twiggs's order to surrender. Instead, he asked to remove troops and property out of the range of state authorities. His reason was a large amount of government stores in El Paso, which he did not want to fall into Confederate hands. But the same Washington ineptness which had impelled Twiggs to surrender also came into play with Fort Bliss, and on March 1, 1861, the garrison surrendered to Confederate troops. Lt. Col. John R. Baylor arrived in June and began making arrangements to smooth over Indian troubles on the frontier (see Chapter 3, "Fort Davis"), even going so far as to host the Mescalero Chief Nicolas at dinner in El Paso.

Meanwhile, the U.S. commander in New Mexico, Col. Edward R. S. Canby was amassing 4,000 men at Fort Craig, to thrust down the river and retake El Paso. However, his plans were changed when Confederates under Gen. H. H. Sibley stabbed into New Mexico in a campaign to conquer the west. Sibley's forces included the garrison at Fort Bliss, which left the post in July 1861 to join the expedition. Following the Confederate defeat at Glorieta Pass on March 28, 1862, retreating Southern troops came back through El Paso and burned the post. A short time later, the city was occupied by U.S. volunteers from California, who remained until the end of the war. Meanwhile, what the Confederates didn't destroy, nature did, as the river eroded much of the Magoffin site.

The Salt Wars

When the military again set about building a permanent post in 1868, it selected Concordia Ranch, about a mile northeast of the Magoffin site. The new location consisted of 100 acres with buildings, all rented by the government.

By 1875 a survey of the Military Division of the Missouri noted no hostile Indians in the vicinity, and the following year, the post was abandoned. But the government reckoned without the lawless element in the area. El Paso became another rough, rowdy frontier town, with the crime—indeed with the local government—under the rule of three major syndicates.

The situation boiled over in 1877. East of El Paso, under the shadow of the Guadalupe Mountains, lies a large salt basin, which for centuries served as a free source of the commodity. Many had tried to lay claim to it before County Judge Charles Howard finally gained control, and assessed charges on all mining and traffic. In the ensuing power struggles, Howard double-crossed two partners, who incited their miners against him.

The dispute soon pitted the Spanish-speaking and English-speaking communities against each other. Troops temporarily stationed in El Paso were dispatched to nearby San Elizario to restore order, only to find the town sealed off. There were kidnappings, riots, and murders. Finally, troops were sent from Fort Davis, and from Fort Bayard and Fort Stanton in New Mexico. An uneasy truce was established, but the soldiers had arrived to stay. In May 1879 Fort Bliss was reactivated.

Border Troubles

By now, the adobe buildings of Concordia had crumbled, so a fourth site was occupied. This, by far was the most strategic location yet, sitting squarely on the actual pass across the river, at a spot known as Hart's Mill. The War Department finally received sufficient funds to declare a reservation, and permanent buildings were constructed.

But if the military wanted the spot, so did the railroads. And in 1881 the railroads won, securing the right-of-way for construction straight across the parade ground. Troops side-stepped Southern Pacific and the Santa Fe as long as they could, but ultimately it became time for another change. In 1893 Fort Bliss was relocated to the fifth site, which it now occupies. Construction commenced on substantial masonry barracks and officers quarters, similar to those fashionable at other U.S. military posts. The original quadrangle of the present post could just as easily be at Fort Sam Houston or at Schofield Barracks, Hawaii.

The area grew quiet in the early years of the twentieth century. Civil order had long since been reestablished in El Paso. Mexico was entering the final years of a long era of peace under the aging Porfirio Diaz. Diaz himself came to Ciudad Juarez, opposite El Paso, where he met President William Howard Taft

A replica of the second Fort Bliss, the Magoffin Ranch site, has been built as a museum on the present, and fifth site. This old artillery caisson is one of several historic military vehicles displayed on the grounds.

in the center of the new bridge linking the two cities. Cavalry from Bliss provided Taft's escort.

But with the collapse of the Porfirian Era, Mexico was again plunged into turmoil. Fighting flared up over much of the border, and artillery was placed on Mount Franklin in El Paso to command Juarez and shell it if necessary. The part of Mexico opposite Fort Bliss was the range of Gen. Francisco Villa, and fighting began to spill over into El Paso. Accordingly, in 1914 Villa met with Brig. Gen. John J. Pershing, the American commander, and agreed to pull back from Juarez.

Two years later, guerillas purportedly attached to Villa raided Columbus, New Mexico. Pershing was ordered to cross the border and hunt him down. But the War Department and the State Department were at odds over which Mexican faction to support. So whether by accident or design, Pershing chased Villa all over the Chihuahua deserts without ever catching him.

Following the Revolution in Mexico and the First World War, the cavalry settled back into what some called the "Polo Period." It was an easy, but expensive life for young officers expected to maintain a string of polo ponies and make regular appearances at the club. Troops did maneuver and train, but some strategists in Washington began to feel the horse soldier's days were numbered. Even so, as war broke out in Europe, it was decided to consolidate the cavalry, and to modernize and intensify its training. Accordingly, in 1940 all regular mounted units were withdrawn to Fort Bliss and consolidated into the 1st Cavalry Division. Two years later, the office of Chief of Cavalry was abolished, and the age of the frontier horse soldier was over.

Fort Bliss Today

As stated, Fort Bliss today is the largest air defense installation in the Western World. In Texas alone, it includes the fort proper, the military reservation, Castner Range, and Biggs Army Airfield. From there, it extends into New Mexico, comprising a total of 1.25 million acres. Entering from Airway Boulevard, the visitor passes row after row of buildings

with signs in German, and trainees wearing the sky blue uniform of the new German Air Force. During my own visit, I met members of Princess Patricia's Light Infantry of the Royal Canadian Armed Forces.

Beyond the German area is an adobe replica of the old Magoffin Ranch post, built in 1948 as a museum by the El Paso Chamber of Commerce. In the yard, a tree has been clipped into the shape of a horse, and is appropriately named "Garryowen." The 1893 Quadrangle, which includes the commanding officer's quarters occupied by Pershing, is now a national historic site. The house used by Field Marshal Bradley during the last years of his life has been dismantled.

The first two sites of Fort Bliss have long since been lost to erosion. The third site is now occupied by Concordia Cemetery, just off I-10. John Wesley Hardin is buried there. The fort at Hart's Mill is located on the U.S. 85 alternate (Paisano Drive), near its intersection with I-10. Preserved are two officers quarters now used as apartment houses, and some old barracks buildings, one of which has been incorporated into a restaurant. A walk of about 100 yards to the restaurant yard takes the visitor to the actual Paso del Norte.

Garryowen, a cavalry horse trimmed from a tree and outfitted with hooves, eyes, and bridle, gallops across the yard of the Old Fort Bliss replica. Buildings of the present post are in the background.

III

THE ADVANCING FRONTIER

As the Texas frontier moved westward, the United States military posture was primarily defensive. At the close of the Mexican War, a string of forts was built at what was then considered the edge of frontier development, on a line running from the Rio Grande to the Trinity River. The southern anchor was Fort Duncan at Eagle Pass on the Rio Grande, with the northernmost post being Fort Worth. Between the two were Forts Inge, Lincoln, Martin Scott, Croghan, Gates, and Graham. On the Nueces, Fort Merrill protected the road between the coastal settlements and San Antonio, and Fort Ewell, the road to Eagle Pass.

However, the frontier expanded before these forts really became useful, and by the end of the 1850s, all but Fort Duncan had been abandoned in favor of a second line farther to the west. This string began with Forts Belknap, Phantom Hill, McKavett, Mason, Terrett, and Clark. The line was later shifted with closures of some posts and establishment of a series of camps and subposts, dictated primarily by geography.

In the mid-nineteenth century, much of Texas was still unexplored. Indeed, mapping would not be completed until the early 1900s, when surveyors from Fort Clark finally filled in the voids. Consequently, several forts of this second line were badly located through sheer ignorance of geography.

However, an east-west line, founded in the late 1840s and early 1850s to protect the road to California, was generally excellently situated. The principal installations on this line were Fort Lancaster, Fort Stockton, Fort Davis, and Fort Bliss, again with secondary forts, subposts, and camps placed according to immediate needs.

Like the river forts, these posts had no actual fortifications, but were open. Barracks, officers' quarters, and administrative buildings generally surrounded a large parade ground, with support buildings, corrals, and stables constructed beyond this quadrangle. In conflict with the basic defensive posture of the times, farsighted military planners determined that soldiers unprotected by walls would be far more likely to seek out and destroy an enemy.

The Camel Corps

The east-west posts went through some of the most rugged and arid country in the Western Hemisphere, leading to a unique experiment in U.S. military history. This was the Camel Corps, established in 1856 at the instigation of Secretary of War Jefferson Davis. The theory was that the terrain was more suited to camels, which would move faster, haul heavier loads, and require less water than horses or mules.

The first herd of military camels arriving at Indianola included 36 adults along with 2 calves born at sea. They were headquartered at Camp Verde, and used along the Western Trail to California. The results were satisfactory, and 41 more were imported. The experiment ended when the United States Army surrendered its installations after Texas left the Union. Such camels as remained were turned loose or sold off.

It has often been said that politics was the reason for the failure of the Camel Corps. After all, Davis served as president of the Confederacy during the War Between the States. In reality, the Camel Corps was no longer needed after the war, due to rapid expansion of railroads and other means of communication. Like the Pony Express, it was obsolete before it really came of age.

Davis has also been accused of using the 2nd Cavalry in Texas as a training ground for officers for the coming war. Admittedly, the 2nd was the most active regiment in Texas during the Indian skirmishes in the 1850s, and a large number of its officers later became leaders in the Confederate Army. However, because of its mobility, the 2nd was best able to deal with superb horsemen such as Kiowas and Comanches. And it must be remembered that the South had traditionally supplied a disproportionately large number of officers to all branches of the United States Army. It is unlikely that Davis was making any plans for a Confederate army during his tenure as U.S. Secretary of War.

Indian Conflicts

The withdrawal of federal troops from Texas and the failure of the Texas Indian reservations (see "Fort Belknap") led to wholesale raiding by the major Indian tribes, particularly Comanches, Kiowas, Lipan Apaches, and Apaches. The Confederate Frontier Battalion, Rangers, and local militia fought a valiant holding action. But with most of the military involved in the war in the East, there was little these troops could do to stop the depredations. Consequently, settlers found it necessary to "fort up," that is, to gather around in a single fortified compound for mutual defense. The largest of these compounds was Fort Davis (not connected with the federal post of the same name), which is commemorated by a marker on the grounds of Fort Griffin State Historic Park.

Ironically, it was an incredible blunder by the Frontier Battalion and state militia which brought the involvement of a previously neutral tribe, the Kickapoos. The troops had first run across the trail of a large party of Indians near the ruins of Fort Phantom Hill. Evidence showed hundreds of people and thousands of horses were in the party. Thinking it to be a major band of Comanches, the soldiers followed until they found the band at Dove Creek in what is now Irion County on January 8, 1865.

In fact, the band was a branch of the Kickapoos, fleeing from Oklahoma to Mexico in the face of advancing white pressure and hoping to avoid a confrontation. Still ignorant of the nature of the band, the soldiers attacked. They found themselves faced with several hundred warriors, armed with modern Lee-Enfield rifles, and familiar with white tactics through long association. The attack was repulsed with 22 whites killed and 19 wounded. Indian losses are not known, but were probably minor. This unwarranted attack earned the Army the hatred of the Kickapoos, who raided from Mexico into Texas from then on, until their power was finally broken by Col. Ranald Mackenzie (see "Fort Clark").

Fort Duncan

In Fort Duncan Park, below the international bridge in Eagle Pass.

Early History

Fort Duncan was located on the Rio Grande, and in later years was more closely tied to Fort McIntosh than with posts in the interior. But it was founded in March 1849 as the southern anchor of the chain of posts built across Texas to guard the Western frontier. And within view of Fort Duncan, the last remaining unit of the Confederate States Army disbanded.

Initially, the fort guarded the trail of California immigrants who worked their way up from Point Isabel, and served as a base of operations against Lipan Apaches. Visiting it in the early 1850s, Frederick Law Olmsted wrote, "The vicinity of the forts is even more dangerous than the unprotected frontier, for the fine horses and arms of the stolid regulars are an exciting attraction for the savages . . . At Fort Duncan such depredations were frequent. A sergeant, who was bringing in a load of hay, was pounced upon, within a mile of the fort, and, before he could rally the muskets of his escort, three mules were cut from the traces under his nose, and jerked into the chaparral."

The Confederate Occupation

As the area grew quiet, Duncan was abandoned in 1859, but regarrisoned the following year because of the Cortina War (see Chapter 2). When Texas left the Union, the post was again abandoned along with other federal installations.

Eventually, the Confederates took the fort over and operated it as Rio Grande Station. Southern troops were in control on February 9, 1864, when Col. Santos Benavides arrived from San Antonio, with word that the post was in danger of attack from renegades across the river in Piedras Negras. The "renegades" were in fact Unionists being recruited for the Federal 1st Texas Cavalry by T. P. McManus. On the day of Benavides's arrival, McManus took a de-

This is the Fort Duncan magazine. The post has been turned into a public health and recreational area.

tachment downriver toward Brownsville, hoping to link up with other Federals he thought were in the area. Benavides started after him, but returned to Fort Duncan after hearing rumors of a possible attack on the adjoining town of Eagle Pass.

The attacks never materialized, but the area remained a point of contention. Several squads of Unionists crossed the river in April, only to be chased back into Mexico. Confederate officials at Duncan complained bitterly to the Mexican commandant, but nothing was done.

On June 17, about 40 Unionist guerrillas crossed the river above Eagle Pass and hoisted the U.S. flag. More came the next day. Capt. James Ware, commander at Fort Duncan had only 34 men and so called out the local militia. The town was barracaded, and guards were set up at key buildings in the fort and in Eagle Pass. The guerrillas attacked that afternoon, overwhelming the defenders in town and capturing Ware and several others. However, at the post hospital, soldiers and militia dug in and repulsed the invaders. After turning the prisoners loose, the guerrillas retreated back across the river.

Texas in general, and Fort Duncan in particular, may have been far removed from the main theaters of the War Between the States. But the final act of the war was carried out within view of Duncan. On July 4, 1865, Gen. Joseph Shelby's Missouri Cavalry, the last active unit of the Confederate States Army, crossed into Mexico, preferring exile to surrender. On a sandbar in the river, these worn-out troops paused to bury their battle flag. Although the warship Shenandoah was still on the high seas, trying to reach Britain without being caught by the Federal navy, Shelby's act signaled the war was truly over.

Border Troubles

The United States Army returned in 1868, when Lt. Col. William R. Shafter brought units of the 9th Infantry and Headquarters Company of the 41st Infantry to Fort Duncan. For awhile, things were quiet. Then trouble broke out in Mexico, and in 1871, the federal garrison in Piedras Negras was attacked by rebels supporting Porfirio Diaz. The local commander, Col. Pedro Advicula Valdez, called Col. Winker by the Americans, held as long as he could but realized the government position was hopeless without American intervention. To get it, he arranged a lot of random shooting across the river into Fort Duncan. Maj. Zenas Bliss, who by this time commanded the American garrison, sent a note to both sides that he did not plan to intervene. Instead,

he said if the shooting did not stop he would bombard Piedras Negras.

The heavy fighting stopped, and both sides in Piedras settled down to a long siege. By February 1872 Col. Winker had determined that the government position was hopeless. Through a ruse, he tried to divert U.S. forces, so that he could cross with his command into Texas. Then he mounted dummies around the defenses in Piedras Negras and filled every well with dead horses.

But Bliss refused to be bluffed, and when Col. Winker led his forces across the river, they were rounded up and interned in Fort Duncan. There, Col. Winker watched in amusement as the rebel forces began firing at empty fortifications in Piedras. When there was no return fire, they ventured into the city and found it ruined.

A short time later, Bliss paroled Col. Winker to departmental headquarters, so he could go to San Antonio and try and get his men released. But he broke his parole and headed toward Laredo, where he was arrested and detained at Fort McIntosh. When he was released, he recognized that the rebels would win in Mexico and put Porfirio Diaz into power. Pedro Advicula Valdez—Col. Winker—threw in with Diaz. He eventually retired and died on his hacienda in 1885.

At Fort Duncan, troops continued to be occupied with Indians. On August 16, 1870, the Seminole-Negro Scouts were formed at the post. The first group consisted of Sgt. John Kibbitts and ten privates. They signed up for six months with cavalry pay. Later, the Scouts were brought up to 50 men. Army records were none-too-complimentary of them when it came to the usual spit-and-polish. But as combat soldiers, Maj. Bliss called the Scouts "excellent hunters and trailers, and brave scouts . . . splendid fighters."

The unit fared well at Fort Duncan until Christmas 1874, when a shooting broke out in the Blue Goose Saloon between several Scouts, and local gunfighter, King Fisher, and his gang. Shortly thereafter, the Scouts were transferred to Fort Clark.

Fort Duncan troops were active in Col. Ranald Mackenzie's campaigns against the Kickapoos, and in Shafter's mop-up following the Mackenzie victory at Palo Duro (see Chapter 4, "Fort Concho"). In January 1892 Frederic Remington stayed at the post en route to Mexico for some hunting. During his visit, he made sketches for several of his paintings, such as "A Practice March in Texas." By now, however, the post was no longer important. In fact, it had been downgraded to become Camp Eagle Pass. In 1900 Fort Duncan was abandoned.

But the post still had its uses. On March 3, 1911, a Wright biplane carrying Lt. Benjamin D. Foulois and Wright Company exhibition flier Philip Parmalee landed on the old parade ground. They had flown up from Fort McIntosh reconnoitering the river along the way. The 106-mile flight took 2 hours and 10 minutes, and was the first service flight in U.S. military history. Two days later, Foulois and Parmalee took off from Fort Duncan and headed back toward Laredo. But 25 miles downriver, they flew into some ducks and in the excitement, one of the pilots released the engine compression valve. Foulois recranked the engine a few feet above the river, but the sudden thrust threw the plane into the water. Neither pilot was injured, but the plane was badly damaged.

With the Border Troubles in 1916, Fort Duncan was regarrisoned, and it continued in use as a training camp through the First World War. But beyond that, the military had no further need of it. It was maintained as a camp until 1938, when it was turned over to the City of Eagle Pass.

Fort Duncan Today

Today, the Fort Duncan reservation is used for public health and recreation. There are playgrounds and ballfields. A hospital stands on the site of the old post hospital, although the present building is more recent than that used by the military. There are still a number of military buildings used for various purposes, all of which are carefully labeled according to their role when the fort was active. A museum is maintained in the headquarters.

Fort Croghan

In Burnet, on State 29, half a mile west of the intersection with U.S. 281.

Establishment and Construction

Like Fort Duncan, Fort Croghan was one of the first string of forts built by the federal government to protect the Western Frontier immediately following the Mexican War. It was about midway between Duncan and Fort Worth.

The fort succeeded a Ranger camp established near Burnet under Capt. Henry E. McCulloch on December 31, 1847. However, after the federal government authorized the military posts, the Rangers were relieved by Company A of the 2nd Dragoons, in December 1848. The commander of the company, Lt. C. H. Tyler, had planned to build the post on the site of McCulloch's camp. But objections from the property owner, Samuel E. Holland, caused him to move the post to a site three miles away, on a slope of Post Mountain leading down to Hamilton's Creek. Fort Croghan was established there on March 18, 1849, and named for Col. George Croghan, inspector-general, who had died two months earlier.

The initial post consisted of tents and huts. On October 13, 1849, Tyler turned Fort Croghan over to Capt. Arthur T. Lee, in command of Company C, 8th Infantry, and construction of permanent buildings began in earnest.

Noah Smithwick, pioneer settler in Burnet and the fort's first armorer, left a description. "Fort Croggin [sic] consisted of the usual log cabins, inclosed by a stout stockade, and was manned by one company of

This old outpost building on the grounds of Fort Croghan in Burnet was originally located on the other side of Post Mountain from the fort, to give advanced warning of hostiles.

cavalry and one of infantry . . ." Smithwick wrote, adding, ". . .when the commander of Fort Croggin [sic] advertised for an armorer, I went up and worked a short time, long enough, however, to get an inside into the workings of the government machinery. There was a little upstart of a noncommissioned officer, who, having been made a sergeant, appropriated another fellow's wife and put on more airs than did the department commander. He set up a carriage and his wife had to have a servant and fine clothes. As his regular pay would not nearly pay his expenses he made up the deficit by cheating the government."

Smithwick recalled how this particular sergeant asked him to fix the scales so that he could draw extra rations to sell on the black market. And he offered to share the proceeds. Smithwick says he refused.

Although Smithwick's recollection, written years later, leaves the impression of a gigantic stockade surrounding an entire fort as in the John Wayne movies, surveys of the period say differently. Instead, they show the usual open post, with various buildings generally leading to an open drill field/parade ground. The stockade was most likely that surrounding the stables, and it was not impregnable. During the harsh winter of 1852–53, the Indians grew restive, and on one rainy night stole nine good Dragoon horses from the stables. Bvt. Maj. H. H. Sibley, then post commander, took 15 men and chased them as far as Fort Phantom Hill, near Abilene, before turning back.

Indian Wars

Fort Croghan's usefulness was short-lived. Although Indian trouble in the Burnet area lasted into the 1870s, the frontier had pushed farther west. It was felt local problems could be handled by minutemen drawn from area residents.

In his inspection of the post on September 16, 1853, Bvt. Lt. Col. W. G. Freeman reported, "Fort Croghan for some time had been garrisoned by Company I, 2d Dragoons, under Capt. and Bvt. Maj. H. H. Sibley, of that regiment, but recent orders directed the abandonment of the post, and the day before my arrival Maj. Sibley marched for Phantom Hill, with a large train of wagons carrying off most of the property and leaving a small detachment under 1st Lt. N. C. Givens, 2d Dragoons, as a guard until the few stores remaining could be removed."

Givens commanded a detachment of 26 men as guard. There were still several patients in the hospital, so Post Surgeon G. F. Turner stayed until September 23, when he left for Fort Mason. In December the post was permanently abandoned.

Restoration and Present Condition

The government had leased the property on which the post stood for $50 a month. When the military left, the land reverted back to Peter Kerr, the owner. Several tracts were sold off almost immediately and some of the buildings were demolished. Even so, local minutemen used the post to drill and hold rifle practice, and families gathered there during Indian threats. But as civilization became established, the land was parceled out, and one by one the buildings were taken down. One of the most substantial was the post hospital, which was used as a private residence until torn down in 1922. Its logs were sold off as fence posts.

The Burnet County Historical Society managed to obtain 1.7 acres of the old site, including the last remaining military building, a stone structure thought to have been the adjutant's office. The society disbanded and was replaced in 1978 with the Burnet County Historical Commission. The 1.7-acre fort site was deeded to the county, which maintains it as a museum. The museum is closed during the winter.

In addition to the fort structure, several other historic buildings from the area have been relocated to the site. One is a reconstructed stagecoach station from the Hamilton Creek Crossing on the old Austin-Llano Road, which was later used by the local militia. Also on the site is the 1850 Kincheloe log cabin, and a stone house built in the 1850s by Logan Vandeveer, who sold beef to Fort Croghan. A stone and log military outpost has been moved to the museum from its original site on the west side of Post Mountain, where it had been situated to give visibility for miles.

There is also a reconstruction of a period blacksmith shop, containing tools belonging to Noah Smithwick. The Fry log cabin contains a spinning wheel carried on the Runaway Scrape, when Texians fled the advancing armies of Santa Anna after the fall of the Alamo.

Post returns show that eight soldiers died while stationed at Fort Croghan. Most were buried in a little cemetery on Post Mountain, just west of the fort. This cemetery is now lost. One of the eight, a Private Baker, was killed by Indians on the Clear Fork of the Brazos on March 25, 1853, during Sibley's expedition against the hostiles who had stolen the horses. He was probably buried where he died, rather than in the cemetery.

Fort Belknap

A county park on FM 61 between Newcastle and Graham in Young County. The turnoff is marked in Graham.

Establishment and Construction

Only a small corner area remains of the once-vast Fort Belknap. But at its height, the post was the biggest on the Texas frontier, and its establishment led directly to the settlement of Young County. The area was empty when Fort Belknap was founded on June 14, 1851. By the time it closed in 1859, a thriving town had sprung up directly adjacent to the post, and many settlers had moved into the surrounding area. In fact, much of the settlement came from soldiers who remained after they received their discharges.

Fort Belknap was founded by Gen. William Goldsmith Belknap, at that time commander of the Department of Texas, and was part of the second line of frontier defense. Initially named Camp Belknap, it was relocated to a permanent site and upgraded to a fort on November 3 of that year. By the time of Col. Freeman's report (see Chapter 2, "Fort Brown"), not quite two years later, it was headquarters of the Fifth Infantry, with a band and a respectable regimental library.

"There is a considerable quantity of Ordnance at the post, which is well preserved," Freeman wrote. "The Magazine is a substantial structure of stone. The

The Fort Belknap magazine, now a chapel, is one of two original buildings from the post. The rest are reconstructions, primarily dating from the Texas Centennial in 1936, but built of original materials on the orginal foundations.

ordnance consists principally of one 6 pd'r gun, one 12 pd'r howitzer and two 12 pd'r mountain howitzers, all of brass; two 6 pd'r iron guns; 800 rounds of fixed ammunition of various kinds; 550 lbs. of powder; 47,000 musket cartridges, ball and buck; and ten sets of harness."

Freeman reported the beginnings of white settlement in the area, as well as large numbers of Indians. He said there were about 300 Southern Comanches who periodically visited the post. The Red River Comanches also called from time to time "but always in small numbers."

In 1854, Capt. Randolph B. Marcy of Fort Belknap, and Maj. Robert S. Neighbors, the state's special agent for Indian affairs, left the post to explore the headwaters of the Brazos and select possible sites for reservations. The result was one for the Comanches around Camp Cooper in what later became Throckmorton County, and one for the Indians of the Brazos a few miles below Fort Belknap.

Though there were some incidents, Indians in the area were fairly quiet during this period leading up to the War Between the States, and most of the energies at Fort Belknap were spent on development. The post itself was a hub, with roads linking it to Fort Worth, San Antonio, Fort Phantom Hill, and even Fort Riley, Kansas. The Butterfield Overland's route from St. Louis to San Francisco included a station at the post. In short, anyone coming to Texas from the Midwestern states and territories passed through Fort Belknap. Col. Albert Sidney Johnston led his 2nd Cavalry through in 1855, en route from Jefferson Barracks, Missouri, to San Antonio. The unit camped about one mile from Belknap during the last week of December, in one of the coldest winters on record. On December 29, Johnston's wife Eliza noted the temperature was one degree below zero, with sleet. She said she and her family suffered headaches from the charcoal fires and lack of ventilation in the tents. Mrs. Johnston gave very little attention to soldier hardships, but in fact, several died of exposure. Fifty-two horses also froze to death on the picket lines.

Indian and White Hostilities

As the area developed, trouble grew between white settlers and reservation Indians. The town itself had a hotel, several stores, a post office, school, church, Masonic lodge, saloons, district court, and other marks of civilization. There were also substantial farming and stock-raising. Taken together with a large number of Indians, it was only a matter of time before the incidents would begin.

At the center of the storm was Maj. Robert S. Neighbors, the special agent, who had been assigned to the reservations themselves after the original agent, Capt. John R. Baylor, had been discharged. Neighbors respected Indians and their right to a peaceful existence, and spent much of his time heading off potential incidents between whites and reservation tribes. This made enemies, particularly among the Rangers, who viewed their job as one of clearing the area of all Indians. And the disgruntled Baylor spent his time stirring up as much trouble as possible.

In 1858, at Baylor's instigation, 15 whites invaded the Brazos Reservation one night, killing 7 Caddoes and Anadarkos while they slept, and wounding 6 others. The raid shocked both whites and Indians. But by now, Neighbors was losing control, and no effort on either side could head it off. On October 21, the grand jury indicted a reservation Indian for attempted murder of a white. But when the sheriff's posse went to the reservation to make the arrest, government representatives ordered it off. Baylor and his adherents were crying for more blood. Finally troops and artillery from Fort Belknap and Camp Cooper had to be called out to protect the reservation tribes.

Neighbors gave up. Despite his belief in the Indian right to a peaceful existence in Texas, he realized the reservation tribes were no longer safe. In 1859 he led them out of Texas and into reservations in Oklahoma. On September 14, shortly after his return to Texas, he was assassinated on the street in the town of Belknap. In May 1860 his murderer, Edward Cornett was indicted for the crime. However, he never came to trial, and on May 25 was himself found dead. Apparently he was killed by some of Neighbors's friends.

In the end, the town of Belknap suffered from the relocation of the reservation Indians. In 1859 Fort Belknap was closed. Troops were sent to Camp Cooper, leaving only a maintenance detachment behind. And with the possibility of civil war, the Butterfield Overland suspended operations in the area. Deprived of the stage line, and no longer able to trade with soldiers, reservation Indians, or the many civil service employees of the reservation, people began moving away.

The Confederate Occupation

In February 1861 Gen. David E. Twiggs ordered all federal property in Texas turned over to the state government. Maj. William H. Emory arrived to take charge of the maintenance detachment at Fort Belknap, and led it north to Kansas.

The failure of the Texas reservations and the removal of U.S. forces led to the first wide-scale Indian depredations in the area. The Confederate Frontier Battalion stationed at Fort Belknap fought hard, assisted by Tonkawa Scouts. Several vicious battles occurred in the area in 1863 and 1864, the largest being Elm Creek. That raid, one of the worst in Texas history, was fought on October 13, 1864, when 400 to 1,000 Comanches and Kiowas (estimates vary) swept through Young County and attacked Fitzpatrick Ranch on Elm Creek. Seven ranch people and five Rangers were killed. Six women and children and 10,000 head of cattle were captured. Some of the captives were recovered. Others died or disappeared. A couple of months later, a detachment from Fort Belknap located a massive trail which was presumed to be Comanche. It turned out to be Kickapoo, and led to the disaster at Dove Creek (see opening paragraphs, this chapter).

Reconstruction and Restoration

In the spring of 1867, U.S. soldiers of the 6th Cavalry reactivated Fort Belknap. The post by now was in ruins, and a massive reconstruction was necessary. The soldiers stayed for five months until the post was ordered permanently abandoned, and they were transferred to Fort Griffin.

The town of Belknap hung on a little longer. And an effort was made to spur growth by using old government buildings. But with the military gone and the relocation of the county seat to Graham, Belknap was no longer necessary. Now, no trace of the town remains. In 1907 the remains of the soldiers in the post cemetery were transferred to Fort Sam Houston.

Restoration of the fort began in 1936, with the Texas Centennial. Only the walls of the old magazine and the corn house, a storage building for grain and fodder, were still standing. They were stabilized and restored. A total of 15 acres, representing the eastern part of the complete fort, were set aside as a county park. The well was relocated under a brush pile, and foundations of the commissary and two barracks buildings were cleared. Several buildings in Newcastle, constructed out of materials taken from the fort, were purchased and dismantled, and the old stones returned to the post for restoration. The commissary was rebuilt, with the lower floor established as a museum. Two barracks and a kitchen were built on original foundations. In 1976 an archives building was added, where early records are kept under climate-controlled conditions.

The park has many historical markers explaining various functions of the multifaceted post. Across the road is the old cemetery of the town of Belknap, which contains the crypt of Maj. Robert S. Neighbors. A state marker at the crypt tells about his life and work.

Fort Phantom Hill

On private property bisected by FM 600, 14 miles north of Abilene.
Open to the public.

Fort Phantom Hill seems like a made-for-Hollywood name. In fact, it was borrowed for a 1966 hoss opera *Incident at Phantom Hill*, although the story line had nothing to do with the actual post. But the name does conjure visions of incredible loneliness and desolation, and indeed, as one sees the chimneys of the ruined fort rising from the hill in the distance, the fort lives up to its name.

Establishment

Fort Phantom Hill was part of the second line of defense. Although it apparently never received a legal name, and was designated "Post on the Clear Fork of the Brazos," the name Phantom Hill was used on the Freeman report in 1853 (see Chapter 2, "Fort

Brown"). So it did gain some official currency with the military.

Freeman noted its remoteness saying, "Phantom Hill lies 59 miles North East of Fort Chadbourne, the intervening country being mostly open and much of it hilly, though presenting no serious obstacles to wagon travel. There had been no communication between the two posts until very recently, when an officer from Fort Chadbourne (Lt. Dodge) passed over and made a sketch of the route. From having been little used the road was very indistinct and difficult to follow, so much so that the noncommissioned officer [at Fort Chadbourne] furnished me as a guide and who had accompanied the officer originally sent to explore the route, went out of his course, thereby causing a detention of half a day."

The very location of the post was a bureaucratic error. Gen. William Belknap, supervising construction of the post later named for him, ordered a second fort on Pecan Bayou. But the aged, overworked Belknap was dying and was relieved by Gen. Persifor F. Smith. Still ignorant of Texas geography, Smith changed the orders to locate the post on the Clear Fork of the Brazos.

Lt. Col. J. J. Abercrombie arrived at the site on November 14, 1851, and set to work building the fort. Stone was quarried two miles away and used for building the magazine, guardhouse and commissary, and for chimneys for the other buildings. Most structures were built of wood, and Freeman noted they were "of a very inferior character . . . put up by the labor of the troops . . . The officers and soldiers are living in pole huts built in the early part of last year. They are now in a dilapidated condition. The company quarters will, in all probability, fall down during the prevalence of the severe northers of the coming winter."

Water was the main problem at Fort Phantom Hill. Nearby Elm Creek was often dry, and the Clear Fork was brackish. The two well-like structures seen today among the ruins are in fact cisterns. Freeman noted this problem and others in his report, which had absolutely nothing good to say about the post.

"No post visited, except for Fort Ewell, presented so few attractions," he wrote. "It is necessary to haul water for the use of the command upwards of four miles; fuel is brought some five to eight miles from a black jack thicket, and the Commanding Officer reports that during the prevalence of northers (November to April) from eight to twelve teams are frequently required for weeks together to supply the garrison. . . . About thirty acres had been cultivated as gardens but the drought had killed everything. If a good site can be found (as I am told is the case) without throwing the post too much out of line, it would really be a charity to remove the garrison to it."

The restored guardhouse at Fort Phantom Hill.

Decline and Ruin

Comanches visited the post from time to time, as did Lipans, Kiowas, and Kickapoos. But only once was the fort threatened, when about 2,500 Penateka Comanches approached under Chief Buffalo Hump. An eight-foot trench was thrown up around the post, and the artillery, two brass six-pounders were placed on a central parapet reminiscent of the Alamo. Seeing that the post was prepared for an assault, the Comanches passed on.

By autumn 1853 four of the five infantry companies had been withdrawn, although Fort Phantom Hill did receive one company of the 2nd Dragoons. Even so, the fort's importance continued to decline. The command had passed from Lt. Col. Abercrombie to Lt. Col. C. A. Waite, to a major, and finally to a first lieutenant, Newton C. Givens. Givens took command on March 26, 1854, and abandoned the post on April 6. Shortly after the troops left, Fort Phantom Hill was destroyed by fire. The origin of the blaze was never determined, and it is doubtful that anyone cared.

In 1858 the Southern Overland Mail took over the fort as a way station. The stone magazine was utilized as a store house, and a second stone structure, probably the commissary, became a stable. The post was also used as a base by Rangers and by units of the Confederate Frontier Battalion. For awhile in the 1870s, it served as a subpost of Fort Griffin.

Meanwhile, the town of Phantom Hill had grown up around the ruins of Fort Phantom Hill, and became a shipping point for buffalo hides. But the town lost out to Anson as temporary county seat, and an effort to obtain the Texas and Pacific Railroad failed. The town died and little trace remains.

The present owners of Fort Phantom Hill have done a remarkable service by cleaning the ruins and clearly marking each building. The stone magazine stands to the west of the highway, with the post proper to the east. The stone guardhouse has been carefully restored, although the commissary building is only a shell.

Officer's quarters, the adjutant's office, post hospital, blacksmith shop, and company quarters are marked by foundations and chimneys, and labeled with carefully lettered wooden signs. A modern farmhouse stands near the commissary, and the ground is littered with old farm implements, making the ruins particularly photogenic. An excellent brochure is available from the Abilene Convention and Visitors Bureau, P.O. Box 2281, Abilene, Texas, 79604.

Fort McKavett

A state historic site on FM 864 between Sonora and Menard. The turnoff is clearly marked on I-10, about five miles east of Sonora.

A Quiet Beginning

The imposing ruins of the commanding officer's quarters of Fort McKavett almost remind one of the ruins of a Scottish Border castle from Sir Walter Scott. The building was intact as late as 1942, when it was destroyed by fire, and attests to the substantial construction of the post as a whole. In fact, as early as 1853, the Freeman report commented, "The buildings are put up of stone, which is found immediately at hand in great abundance and of a quality easily dressed."

Health problems were sufficient for inclusion in the report, in part attributed to the use of soldier labor in construction, there being no civilian workers available. Not only did excess labor without rest periods create health problems, but Freeman felt the troops had insufficient time to drill. Still the soldiers not only continued to work on Fort McKavett, they also cut shingles to send to Fort Chadbourne.

There appears to have been little real problem with hostiles in the area around Fort McKavett prior to the War Between the States. Troops did make patrols and occasionally engaged in punitive expeditions. Throughout the mid-1850s there were some depredations which became particularly acute in the winter and spring of 1855. In March 1855 units from Forts Belknap, Chadbourne, and McKavett were ordered to seek out and destroy any Indians threatening the white settlements. But the threat died down in 1856, when the various hostile bands agreed to go on the reservations (see "Fort Belknap").

With the San Saba Valley quiet in the vicinity of Fort McKavett, white settlers began to move in. Such Indian trouble as existed was in the north, and state and local authorities appeared sufficient for the San Saba. In view of this, Gen. David Twiggs ordered Fort McKavett abandoned on February 5, 1859. The following month, the garrison consisting of Companies C and F of the 1st Infantry marched out for Camp Cooper.

There is no evidence that Confederate or state troops used Fort McKavett during the War Between the States. Instead, the post buildings were occupied

The ruined commanding officers quarters of Fort McKavett resemble the ancient Border castles of Sir Walter Scott. The house was built so substantially that it was still used until 1942, when it burned.

by pioneer families. When U.S. forces came back after the war, they came to pacify white Texans rather than Indians, so residents of the McKavett area banded together with citizens from as far away as Mason to form a Minuteman company for local defense.

The Command of Ranald Mackenzie

By the time the Army reoccupied the post, on April 1, 1868, all the buildings except the commanding officer's quarters had fallen into disrepair, and the soldiers had to live in tents. Troopers of the 4th Cavalry began the long process of reconstruction, augmented later by three companies of the 38th Infantry (Colored). Discipline was a problem, particularly with the formation of a parasite settlement which came to be called Scabtown, across the San Saba River from the post. The pitfalls of Scabtown are shown in a display in the visitors center, located in the post hospital. It follows the case of a single black soldier at Fort McKavett, through court-martial after court-martial. When the display begins, he is a sergeant. When it ends, he has lost all his stripes, forfeited large amounts of pay and served guardhouse time.

Scabtown remained a problem, but discipline took an upswing in 1869, when Col. Ranald S. Mackenzie arrived to take command of the 38th Infantry in 1869. He immediately set about making it one of the most efficient black units in the Army. On September 1, 1869, the 38th was amalgamated with the 41st Infantry, to form the 24th Infantry. Together with the 25th Infantry and the 9th and 10th Cavalry, the 24th was part of the famed Buffalo Soldiers, the black troops who distinguished themselves so brilliantly during the Indian Wars.

Mackenzie was absent much of his time in command at Fort McKavett. The time he spent at the post was used to whip the troops into shape and reconstruct the facilities. A conflict over back rent arose with the owners of the land on which the fort was located, and Mackenzie recommended a permanent reservation be purchased. The government responded by ordering the rent be paid. Mackenzie also got into a dispute with Gen. J. J. Reynolds, commander of the Department of Texas, which lasted several years until Reynolds finally brought charges. A convening board threw them out.

In 1870 Mackenzie was called to Washington for special duty. When he returned, he was commander of the 4th Cavalry at Fort Concho. Command of the 24th Infantry went to his protégé, Lt. Col. William R. Shafter, who apparently also held simultaneous command at Fort Concho.

The Indian Wars

Fort McKavett's primary function in the 1870s was support for large-scale Indian operations waged primarily from posts located closer to the main action. It provided scouts, troops, and supplies in Mackenzie's wars against the Kiowas, Comanches, and Kickapoos, and in operations against the Apaches. There were still come hostiles in the immediate San Saba area, however, and occasionally McKavett's scouts made significant contributions. On May 20–21, 1871, a 9th Cavalry patrol led by Sgt. Emmanuel Stance engaged Indians 3 times and captured 14 horses. For this and similar actions, the diminutive Stance received the Congressional Medal of Honor.

Shafter himself, now in command at Fort Concho, returned to McKavett in July 1870 to mount a major expedition to hunt down hostile camps. Leaving Fort McKavett on August 27, his group rendezvoused with units from Fort Clark and Fort Duncan. But a search of the Pecos and Devil's River regions yielded nothing. Heading back to Fort McKavett, however, Shafter ran across a large abandoned camp. Expeditions like this provided the Army with information for surveillance work, which ultimately helped deny Indians their bases of operation.

Decline and Restoration

With the defeat of hostiles in the close of the 1870s, Fort McKavett declined in importance. In 1882, 30 years after the fort's founding, the main body of troops marched out. A small detachment remained to dispose of government property and turn the buildings over to civilian owners. On June 30, 1883, Company D of the 16th Infantry left, and the post was closed for good. Scabtown, officially the town of Fort McKavett, lingered for awhile, but by and large, it has shrunken to a few houses, a well-kept cemetery, a general store, and a post office.

As they had done in 1859, civilians moved into the post buildings after the Army left. Consequently, many remained in a reasonably good state of repair. Today Fort McKavett State Historic Site contains 14 restored buildings, including officer's quarters, barracks, school, bakery, and headquarters. As stated, the hospital building contains a visitors center with an excellent display on the history of the post. A half-mile hike takes visitors down the hill past the old military limekiln, to the springs which supplied water to the post.

Persons desiring further information may write Park Superintendent, Fort McKavett State Historic Site, P.O. Box 867, Fort McKavett, Texas, 76841.

Fort Clark

On U.S. 90 near the junction with State 131, at the southern edge of Brackettville.

Establishment

Fort Clark remained in service longer than any other post in the Western line of defense. Founded in 1852, it was permanently abandoned in 1946.

Part of its success was in its excellent location. Inspecting it in 1853, Bvt. Lt. Col. Freeman wrote (see Chapter 2, "Fort Brown"), "The post is situated on the west side of the Las Moras River, within 200 yards of its head spring, and about 6 miles south of the Las Moras mountain, which rises to an elevation of some 500 feet above the surrounding country . . . I regard Fort Clark as a point of primary importance, being the limit of arable land in the direction of El Paso, and from its salient position looking both to the Rio Grande and Indian frontiers."

In 1857 Lt. John B. Hood rode into Fort Clark after a five-week sortie against hostiles, which had begun in the area of Fort Mason (see Chapter 6, "Fort Mason"). During the War Between the States, Fort Clark was held by Confederate and state troops, as protection from Indians and bandits, and to guard against any effort at a Unionist invasion from Mexico.

Indian Campaigns of Colonel Mackenzie

But the greatest activity from the post was in the Indian campaigns of Col. Ranald S. Mackenzie (see Chapter 4). In his campaigns against the Comanches, the post served as a source of troops and supplies. However, Fort Clark was the assembly point for Mackenzie's onslaught against the Kickapoos, and subsequently served as his refuge.

Mackenzie had served briefly at Clark before being given full regimental command at Fort McKavett in March 1869. He returned in 1873, summoned by Gen. Philip Sheridan and Secretary of War W. W. Belknap.

In a meeting with Sheridan, Belknap, and Col. Wesley Merritt, Mackenzie was told Kickapoos and Apaches were raiding the countryside, then retreating to a group of villages around Rey Molina, about 60 miles into Mexico. He was expected to do something about it.

The implication was clear. Mackenzie was to invade a friendly foreign power, thus putting the United States at risk of war. Such an order could only have come from the highest level—from President U.S. Grant himself. When Mackenzie asked for written orders, Sheridan pounded the table and shouted, "Damn the orders! Damn the authority! You are to go ahead on your own plan of action, and your authority and backing shall be General Grant and myself. With us behind you in whatever you do to clean up this situation, you can rest assured of the fullest support. You must assume the risk. We will assume the final responsibility, should any result."

On the night of May 17, 1873, Mackenzie led almost 400 men across the Rio Grande. The objective had to be achieved and the troops back home before Mexican authorities had time to react. Shortly after midnight, the pack train fell out, to allow more rapid progress.

The sun was high in the sky when the column reached Rey Molina. Nevertheless, the troops charged straight through, achieving total surprise. They swept the length of three villages, maintaining continuous gunfire and scattering the inhabitants. Then they wheeled about and charged again. After several such charges, the soldiers dismounted, wrecked the food stores and burned the villages.

Then began a mad dash for the border. The country was up in arms. Not only did Mackenzie have to fear the Mexican military, but the local population as well. Tired and hungry, the soldiers began to doze in their saddles. A rear guard was assigned to prod the

A cavalry horse and company guidons **mark the entrance** to Fort Clark, just outside Brackettville.

stragglers along. When the troops recrossed the Rio Grande on May 19, they had ridden 160 miles in 32 hours without food or sleep.

Fort Clark was put on full defensive footing, to repel a possible retaliatory strike by Mexico. The Mexican government itself was in an uproar, and for awhile, war seemed inevitable. The Grant Administration threw up its hands in dismay, then stalled any action until the incident lost importance.

This was the most outstanding of several raids made across the river. Not only did they destroy the hostile bases, but they also convinced the Mexican government to step up its own operations against the Indians. With both armies in the field, the middle border grew quiet.

The Seminole-Negro Scouts

After an incident at Fort Duncan where they were organized, the Army's Seminole-Negro Scouts were transferred to Fort Clark, where they remained until their branch of service was disbanded. These were descendants of Florida Seminoles and runaway slaves, and were among those who had been shipped west during the general clearances of the Eastern states. For the most part, they looked black, but they had certain Indian traits, particularly as trackers.

For nine years beginning in 1873, the Scouts were under Lt. John L. Bullis. During that period, they were in 12 major engagements and 14 minor ones, without the loss of a single man to Indian action. In one fight with Comanches in 1875, the outnumbered Scouts retired from the field. But one of them, Sgt. John Ward, saw Bullis surrounded and cut off from his horse. While two others held off the Indians, Ward grabbed Bullis and took him away on his own horse. All three Seminole-Negroes were later awarded the Congressional Medal of Honor.

Routine Duty

In spite of these actions, much of the duty at Fort Clark was routine, with dust, heat, and vermin being the primary concerns. Frances Anne Boyd, whose husband Orsemus B. Boyd was a lieutenant in the 9th Cavalry at Fort Clark, wrote the temperature was 110 degrees in the shade. "Ice was an unknown luxury. We had nothing for cooling purposes except the ollas, made of porous earth by the Mexicans.

"The post was one hundred and thirty-five miles from San Antonio, the nearest point where anything except absolute essentials could be obtained; and as

stages were the only means of transportation, charges were exorbitant." Mrs. Boyd went on to describe oily butter, dry beef, bad tasting milk, and rotten potatoes. "Fort Clark eventually became very dear to me;" she admitted, "but the first two years were exceedingly trying, for I had to accustom myself anew to fresh modes in every direction."

By 1905 the frontier had grown quiet and relations with Mexico were cordial. The Army devoted its time to surveying the vast, still unknown reaches of Texas. Since there were no officers in Texas available for the job, posts elsewhere were asked to send qualified young officers to Fort Clark. One of them was Lt. George C. Marshall, later general of the army and secretary of state.

Marshall was assigned the area around Del Rio and Langtry, at that time a waterless wasteland. His squad left Fort Clark in June, with such food as it could pack, and an understanding with the quartermaster department that additional food and forage would be shipped to points along the railroad between Del Rio and Sanderson. But there was the usual military foul-up, and provisions were not sent. Marshall reached Langtry in late July, where his men drew pay but no rations. He bought provisions, paying with vouchers, which were subsequently rejected by the government.

By the time he had finished with his sector, Marshall said, "we darn near starved. . . ." But at departmental headquarters in Fort Sam Houston, the chief engineer told him his map not only was the best, but the only one complete.

Modern History

Fort Clark continued to be garrisoned by regular cavalry until 1940. Lt. Gen. Jonathan Wainwright commanded Fort Clark prior to being sent to the Philippines, where he distinguished himself by his defense of Corregidor. When the regulars were sent to Fort Bliss in 1940, the post was turned over to mounted units of the Texas National Guard. In 1946 Fort Clark was closed and the reservation put up for sale.

Fort Clark is now a private country club-condominium resort. Because of this, even some of the oldest buildings are in an excellent state of preservation. The only distraction is the country club style of landscaping around the post, including the parade ground. A museum is maintained at the guardhouse. Due to the fact that the post is now private property, permission must be obtained to drive into the area. Passes are available from the security office at the entrance to the post.

Fort Lancaster

A state historic site near the Pecos River in Crockett County. Take the scenic loop of U.S. 290 off I-10. The post is 10 miles east of Sheffield.

Even today, the ruins of Fort Lancaster are among the most desolate in Texas. At the time of my visit, I was all alone except for a pronghorn that took off when I startled it on the parade ground. A sign warns of rattlesnakes. The park ranger showed up after awhile. He had his and his father's hunting trophies on the wall of the visitors center, and we talked about hunting. It was appropriate, since the only other sounds were shotguns ringing in the surrounding hills.

Key Outpost

But 130 years ago, it was a different story. Fort Lancaster was a lonely post then, too, but the federal government considered it a key point on the Western trails. In his 1856 inspection report, Col. J. K. F. Mansfield wrote, "This post is indispensable to travellers and in a locality often visited by the wild Indians traversing the country. It cannot be dispensed with. At this place, travellers can rest and recruit their ani-

mals and repair their wagons with safety. It undoubtedly has and will save many valuable lives."

Fort Lancaster was a true Indian War post, in the finest traditions of movie director John Ford. "Indians in this locality are marauding parties of Apaches & Mescaleros as highway men, and murderers," Mansfield wrote. "They keep out of sight & commit depredations & murders at times when least expected. They are on the Pecos, in the mountains, on Devils river, &c, always concealed and difficult to find. The night after I left Capt. Linsday at the 1st crossing on his return from Devils river, say 80 miles from Fort Clark, I encamped at the 2d crossing, and a large cow & calf train bound for New Mexico, which was encamped 5 miles ahead of me, was attacked & one man killed & another badly wounded & they were so disorganized when I came up to them in the morning having but 4 men left, as to make it necessary to detach 5 of my escort to accompany them to Camp Lancaster . . . But for my timely arrival, and the aid of this post, these men would have been murdered & their cows & calves, so important to the inhabitants of New Mexico, captured by the Indians."

The remains of a wagon and the bones of a draft ox show the hazards which faced an unwary traveller in West Texas 120 years ago. The display is behind the visitors center at Fort Lancaster.

It was to provide this type of protection and assistance that Fort Lancaster was founded at the midway point between Fort Davis and Fort Clark on August 20, 1855. Initially called Camp Lancaster before being upgraded to a fort, it was garrisoned by Companies H and K of the 1st Infantry. The preliminary post consisted of tents, jacales or picket houses, and Turnley barracks, a nineteenth-century version of the Quonset hut. These were gradually replaced by stone and adobe, until the fort had a substantial number of permanent buildings. Supply was a problem since the post was so remote, and Mansfield noted flour destined for Lancaster had spoiled en route.

In July 1857, when the first train of Jefferson Davis's Camel Corps stopped there for two days, Capt. S. D. Carpenter of Company H took a ride on one of the strange beasts and decided he liked it better than a mule. Thereafter, Lancaster received camels from time to time, as long as the corps existed.

Indian Wars

When Texas left the Union, the troops at Fort Lancaster were ordered to abandon the post. They left for San Antonio on March 19, 1861. Thereafter, the 2nd Texas Mounted Rifles garrisoned it for awhile, as did members of the W. P. Lane Rangers. One of the Rangers lies buried in the post cemetery.

After the Rangers pulled out, Fort Lancaster was abandoned more or less permanently, and started falling into ruin. At some point during the War Between the States the post was burned, most likely by Indians. When Company K of the 9th Cavalry arrived in the fall of 1867, only ruins remained. No major reconstruction was undertaken, since the post was primarily intended to be a bivouacking area. Some

buildings seem to have been partially dismantled and the materials used to upgrade others.

The 9th Cavalry was to distinguish itself during the Indian Wars. But in December 1867 the regiment was only nine months old and had never been in combat. On December 26 Company K was attacked at Fort Lancaster by 900 to 1,200 Kickapoos and Lipan Apaches. The Indians surrounded the post on all four sides. One group of Indians made for the horses, capturing three herd guards. The others attacked the fort. Capt. William Frohock organized a defense, and the troops dug in. After three hours, the attack was thrown back. A corporal shot a man who appeared to have been a chief, but it was unknown whether that Indian was killed or wounded. The fort's only casualties were the herd guards, whose remains were found three months later. The 9th had passed its first test in combat. But before long, Fort Lancaster was again abandoned.

In 1968 the ruins were designated a state historic site. Just beyond the visitors center, by the entrance to the ruins are the remains of a wagon with the bones of its draft ox. These show what pioneers faced in crossing West Texas. The ruins themselves are no more notable than ruins of other Texas posts. However, because of its abandonment, there was little rebuilding or alteration, so that the layout of Fort Lancaster is more clearly defined. Areas which have vanished from other posts, such as the sinks, corral, and laundresses quarters can be easily traced.

The post cemetery still has some of the early headstones. One grave may be that of the three herd guards of the 9th, who died after the December 26 raid. Next to the headstone of one of the Lane Rangers is another stone, inscribed "Little Margaret." Contrary to the television image of the tough pioneer youth, the frontier was hard on children, and the memoirs of many soldiers and their wives contain references to children who died during Western service.

Fort Stockton

On Fifth Street, just west of U.S. 285 in Fort Stockton.

These three houses are all that remain of officers row at Fort Stockton. The center house is being renovated as a museum of the period.

Next to the river forts, which covered fords or faced large Mexican garrisons, it is hard to imagine a post more strategically situated than Fort Stockton. Unusual as it may seem in view of the usual haphazard military way of locating forts, the site was perfect. It was squarely on the Great Comanche War Trail, its guns covering the great springs which Indians had used since prehistoric times. In fact, the springs made Stockton the crossroads of such trails as the San Antonio-Chihuahua, the upper and lower San Antonio-San Diego Mail Routes, and the Butterfield Overland.

Establishment

Fort Stockton was founded in December 1858 by a squad of 20 men drawn from the 1st and 8th Infantry. An adobe post was built and named Camp Stockton, in honor of a naval officer, Commodore Robert Field Stockton, who had assisted with the occupation of California during the Mexican War.

With the removal of U.S. forces from Texas, Fort Stockton was abandoned in May 1861. Confederates held it briefly, but stepped-up Apache raids in the area stretched their resources beyond the limit. The post was burned and abandoned.

On July 4, 1867 the area was reoccupied by units of the 9th Cavalry and 24th Infantry, who set about building a new post a few hundred yards northeast of the original site. The military presence settled the Indians in the immediate area, and an 1874 survey of the Military Division of the Missouri notes no Indians "in the vicinity." It added, "Roving bands of Apaches in small parties from the Guadalupe Mountains often depredate on the highways and lower settlements."

By then, Fort Stockton had grown to 960 acres rented by the government for the post proper, with another 25 acres 3 miles away used as a garden. Impressions of the post were written by Emily K. Andrews, who passed through Fort Stockton with her husband in August 1874, en route to Fort Davis, where he was to take command. "The lack of shade and want of grass, on the Parade make a glare as you look upon it almost intolerable, and we found many of the officers suffering from the effect of it on the eye. They, and also their wives, I found the most agreeable, cultivated people, and sitting chatting in their pleasant parlors, I could easily fancy myself in Boston again . . . I found it quite the fashion at the Post for the ladies to go with their husbands to the billiard room, so one evening we all went by invitation to see them play. The room was in a long adobe building, with a fine table in it and everything very nice. A Mexican Band was playing at one end, and some of the ladies and gentlemen danced while the game was going on."

Apache Wars

Within two years of the survey's comment on Indians, and of Mrs. Andrew's peaceful trip through Fort Stockton to Fort Davis, the Trans-Pecos erupted when the Mescalero Apaches began leaving the Fort Stanton Reservation on raiding parties. By 1878 a full-scale war was underway, led by the Warm Springs Apache Chief Victorio. Many times, troops from Fort Stockton and Fort Davis would trail the Indians back to Fort Stanton, only to be put off by the agent, who insisted his charges were not involved.

To subdue the hostiles, Col. Benjamin H. Grierson was sent to command the newly formed District of the Pecos at Fort Concho. There he set up a series of subposts to blanket the area. Two were maintained by

the garrison at Fort Concho, and three each by Forts Stockton and Davis. Those assigned to Stockton were at Rainbow Cliffs, Frazier's Ranch, and Escondido. So thoroughly was the area covered that by 1879, patrols from Frazier's Ranch covered almost 5,000 miles in just under 4 months, without finding any sign of Indians.

The area around Fort Stockton itself was becoming settled. Like other posts, it spawned a town. Unlike most others, however, this one was not a wide-open frontier den of iniquity. It was made up of solid German, Irish, and Mexican settlers, who tapped the springs to raise crops. Even the name was different. The town was known as St. Gall. It did not become Fort Stockton until an election officially changed the name in August of 1881.

By then the military post's days were numbered. Pecos County had been created in 1875, with St. Gall/Fort Stockton as county seat. By 1877 settlers had 8,000 acres under cultivation. With the end of the Victorio War in 1881, the Army was no longer necessary.

Abandonment and Restoration

In 1884 the government prepared to move the garrison to Fort Davis. However, this was cancelled because adequate barracks at Davis were not ready. Area citizens also worried about whether peace would be maintained once the soldiers left. But in 1886 Fort Stockton was abandoned.

The only trace of the military post is three officers' houses and the guardhouse, around a clearly defined parade ground. The officers' houses are not presently open to the public, although the middle one is being restored to the 1877 fort period. A building on the far side of the parade, on Spring Drive is marked as the post hospital, but is actually the Rollins-Sibley House, built in 1903 on the hospital foundations.

The guardhouse is open, and contains a jailer's quarters, holding cell, and solitary confinement cell. The holding cell has chains shackled to the wall, hanging down against modern grafitti. The solitary cell is a black dungeon.

The old military cemetery is just off Water Street near the intersection with U.S. 290, and was used from 1859 until 1912. After the fort closed, however, remains of the 56 soldiers interred there were moved to Fort Sam Houston.

Fort Davis

A national historical site administered by the United States Department of the Interior at the town of Fort Davis, on State 17, 36 miles south of I-10.

Every hour, bugles echo across the parade ground of Fort Davis. Orders are shouted, the band plays and the Order of the Day is read. It is a recording of the retreat ceremony held at the fort in 1875, when word was received of the death of former President Andrew Johnson. The recording was made at Fort Sill, Oklahoma, by the bands of the 77th and 97th Divisions.

This indicates the importance of Fort Davis in modern times, both as a relic of the past, and in memory of its own major role in westward expansion. Just as it was in frontier days, the post is a showpiece.

Fort Davis sits squarely on the Overland Trail, and was established to provide protection and a stopping point for Westbound travelers. It continued to be a focal point of Indian containment and suppression for almost 30 years, until the surrounding mountains were finally cleared of Apaches.

Stage lines used the fort regularly, with competition so fierce that coaches ultimately came through biweekly. Fort Davis also served as a major stopping point for the Camel Corps.

Establishment

Prior to the establishment of Fort Davis, there was no military protection whatever between Fort Clark and Fort Bliss. In September 1854 the commander of the Department of Texas, Bvt. Maj. Gen. Persifor F. Smith, left San Antonio to inspect the Trans-Pecos area and select a site for the new post. The commander-designate, Lt. Col. Washington Seawell, took six companies of the 8th Infantry, and met Smith at Painted Comanche Camp on Limpia Creek on Oc-

As originally constructed, **Fort Davis was surrounded** on three sides by the walls of Limpia Canyon, causing its first commander to complain that Indians hiding in the rocks could shoot down into the post. (Harper's Magazine, Author's Collection)

Ruins of the barracks of the original Fort Davis are situated behind officers quarters of the later post. Fort Davis was originally built inside Limpia Canyon (background), leaving it in danger of attack from above. After the War Between the States it was moved to a prairie at the mouth of the canyon.

tober 7. After examining a site at Presidio, Smith returned to the Limpia, convinced it was the best location. There was water and forage, and it was within striking distance of the Mescalero Apaches and the Great Comanche War Trail.

The site chosen was surrounded on three sides by Limpia Canyon. The post was founded on October 23, and named for Secretary of War Jefferson Davis. The property was leased from John James of San Antonio for $300 a year, with the War Department retaining an option to purchase—one it never used.

As post commander, Seawell disliked the spot as being too exposed to sudden assault or sniper fire by hostiles hidden in the canyon walls. He would have preferred to build the fort on a plain at the mouth of the canyon, where visibility was better, and fresh water more readily available. But Smith's word was final, and construction got underway. Logs were brought from nearby mountains, a sawmill was established, and buildings went up made from pine slabs set vertically in the ground. They soon began to deteriorate, and subsequent inspectors found many of the quarters unfit for habitation.

The lot of the troops improved, but the location problem was aggravated in 1855, when Seawell was detached on court-martial duty. During his absence, Capt. Arthur T. Lee ordered construction of six stone barracks, 30 by 60 feet, with flagstone floors, thus fixing the post permanently inside the canyon.

Indian Campaigns

No sooner was the post founded than Gen. Smith was back in San Antonio, planning to utilize it in a major campaign against the Mescaleros. The expedition consisted of three companies of the Mounted Riflemen, three companies of state militia, and one company of 8th Infantry. Although the campaign lasted three months, there were only a few engagements. But the intensive scouting forced many Indians into New Mexico, where other troops rounded them up and confined them to the reservation at Fort Stanton.

Scattered bands continued to harass the San Antonio-El Paso Road, requiring posts at Fort Lancaster, Fort Stockton, Camp Hudson, and Fort Quitman. A mail escort out of Fort Lancaster was attacked in the summer of 1856, forcing the outnumbered soldiers to abandon the wagons and withdraw to Lancaster. The Fort Davis post returns for the first quarter of 1857 were destroyed when another mail escort was attacked and four of the seven soldiers were killed.

On July 24, 1857, the military express from San Antonio to Fort Davis was attacked just west of the Pecos River. The escorting infantrymen retreated to Fort Lancaster, where they met a detachment of 40 men from Fort Davis, under command of Lt. Edward Hartz. Hartz loaded his men into covered wagons, then set out for Davis disguised as a provision train.

The Indians attacked 45 miles west of Fort Lancaster. Suddenly the covers of the wagons were drawn up and the soldiers opened fire. Surprised and shaken, the Indians rode out of range and set fire to the prairie grass. Hartz pulled the wagons into a depression to avoid the flames, then advanced against the Indians again. The war party broke up and fled.

That same year, the Camel Corps made its first appearance at Fort Davis, en route to Arizona to survey a road. In 1859 the camels were back, this time for a dual purpose—to find a shorter route from San Antonio, and to test the durability of 24 camels compared with 24 mules, both teams loaded to capacity. Lt. Hartz, who had scattered the Indians with his dummy wagon train, commanded the escort. The camels passed this test and a much more severe one the following year. This was their last project however, because in 1861, Texas left the Union and the Camel Corps headquarters at Camp Verde was seized by the Confederates.

Confederate Occupation

With secession came the order to abandon Texas posts. On April 13, 1861, the garrison at Fort Davis met those from Fort Bliss and Fort Quitman and marched east to surrender. In June the Confederate 2nd Texas Mounted Rifles arrived under the command of Lt. Col. John R. Baylor. Baylor seems to have mellowed since his deadly quarrel with Maj. Robert Neighbors (see "Fort Belknap"), and established cordial relations with the Mescalero Chief Nicolas. One company of the 2nd Texas left at Fort Davis enjoyed peace and quiet for two months, until Nicolas raided the post for horses.

Lt. Reuben Mays took fourteen men and followed the trail into the Big Bend. There, the Confederates were ambushed and massacred. The only survivor was the Mexican scout.

In spite of this, Confederate strategy was directed at securing New Mexico, and no effort was made to stop the Apaches. Realizing this, the Indians stepped up their depredations, so that the area was no longer safe. Meanwhile, Gen. H. H. Sibley had penetrated New Mexico, and Fort Davis had become a receiving station for the wounded. But with the defeat at Glorieta Pass in March 1862, Southern hopes in the West were dashed. Pursued by the U.S. California Volunteers, the Confederates abandoned the Trans-Pecos.

The first black graduate of West Point, Lt. Henry O. Flipper was assigned to the 10th Cavalry at Fort Davis. His haphazard handling of military funds brought charges of embezzlement and dismissal from the service. Years after his death, he was exonerated of any wrongdoing. (Courtesy of the U.S. Military Academy Archives.)

On August 27, 1862, Company C of the 1st California Cavalry under Capt. E. D. Shirland rode into Fort Davis. Recalling the event, John C. Cremony wrote, "Upon Shirland's arrival he found the fort deserted by the Confederates; but also discovered they had left three men behind who had been seized with small-pox. Those poor fellows were abandoned to their fate; but the Confederate troops had scarcely left the place before the Apaches arrived, and with their usual caution they made careful inspection before trusting themselves into the building. In the course of their investigations they discovered the three sick men, and recognizing the disease with which they were afflicted, filled their bodies full of arrows shot from between the iron bars of the windows; and without attempting to enter the fortress, went on their way toward their own fastness. A few days afterward, Shirland, at the head of twenty-five men, encountered over two hundred of those same Apaches at the place known as 'Dead Man's Hole,' and killed twenty-two of them without sustaining any other loss than that of a single carbine."

Intermittent Peace

Over the next five years, Fort Davis fell into ruin, inhabited only by squatters and renegades. Finally, on June 29, 1867, Lt. Col. Wesley Merritt led four troops of the 9th Cavalry to reactivate the post. Since the old buildings were virtually useless, Merritt began construction of a new fort beyond the mouth of the canyon, where Col. Seawell had wanted it 13 years before. Construction continued as the need arose and money became available for over 15 years, until the mid-1880s, when Fort Davis assumed its final form.

Military duties accompanied construction. The garrison patrolled the roads to Fort Quitman and Fort Stockton, and guarded mail stations along the route. In 1868, about 200 Apaches raided a train near Fort Stockton and headed toward the Big Bend and Mexico. Merritt sent 60 soldiers of the Ninth along with 10 volunteers, who ran the hostiles down in the Santiago Mountains and won a major victory. Two captive Mexican children were recovered.

In 1869 Merritt was relieved by Col. Edward Hatch, a tough aggressive soldier, who subscribed to the policy of seek out and destroy. On Jan. 20, 1870, a detachment overran a camp in the Guadalupe Mountains and killed about 25 hostiles. Two more expeditions were sent out the same year, maintaining pressure against the Indians and driving them from the Guadalupes.

The Warm Springs Apache Chief Victorio unified his people with the Mescaleros, and created havoc in the Trans-Pecos for several years prior to his death in Mexico in 1880. (Courtesy of the National Archives.)

Hatch was succeeded by Lt. Col. William R. Shafter, whose own aggressive tactics in West Texas earned him the name Pecos Bill. In the summer of 1871 he led a detachment in pursuit of a Comanche raiding party across the Monahans Sands, a desolate area of bare dunes which whites had previously avoided. The expedition also penetrated the Staked Plains, putting the Indians on notice that nowhere in Texas was safe. From the Staked Plains, Shafter turned his attention to the Big Bend. By September 1871 the Indians had enough and began turning themselves in at the Fort Stanton Reservation.

For four years, the Trans-Pecos was reasonably quiet. Then in 1876 the Apaches broke loose again. In 1876 and again in 1877, people were murdered practically on the Fort Davis perimeter. Once more the road from Davis to El Paso was unsafe. But the depredations had taken a new turn. Previously, the Indians' main interest had been thievery. Now, they had turned to murder raids.

In 1878 the departmental commander, Brig. Gen. Edward O. C. Ord, formed West Texas into the District of the Pecos, with Col. Benjamin Grierson in command at Fort Concho. The area was covered with subposts (see "Fort Stockton"). Troopers from the three subposts of Fort Davis scouted 6,724 miles in 1878 alone, pressuring the Indians and gaining new information about the area.

The Victorio Wars

The frontier appeared to be settling down again, when Victorio, chief of the Warm Springs Apaches,

combined his warriors with dissatisfied Indians from the Mescalero agency and went to war. The combined Warm Springs-Mescalero group tore through New Mexico, before crossing the border to safety in Mexico proper.

It wasn't long before Victorio was back, making off with 46 horses from a troop of the 9th Cavalry, and generally creating mayhem for the military. Unbeaten, he and his Warm Springs band became a rallying point for the Mescaleros. A brilliant tactician, he lured a group of Mexican volunteers from Carrizal, Chihuahua, into an ambush and massacred them. Then he massacred every member of a relief party.

For once, Mexico and the United States joined forces against a common enemy. In the United States, Col. Hatch, who now commanded troops in New Mexico, felt Victorio was drawing support from the Fort Stanton Reservation. Two columns from New Mexico and one from Texas met at the reservation on April 12, 1880. Approaching from the west, Hatch attacked a group of Victorio's band and found agency tags on them.

At Stanton, the reservation Indians resisted being disarmed. Grierson's 10th Cavalry charged and rounded up most of the hostiles. Perhaps as many as 50 managed to escape to Victorio, who again fled to Mexico.

Grierson concentrated eight troops of the 10th Cavalry at Fort Davis, which would serve as base of operations for a major offensive. From there, he strengthened the subposts of Viejo Pass, Eagle Springs, and Fort Quitman. He was at Quitman on July 28, when he learned Victorio had again crossed the river.

The following day Grierson left Fort Quitman with a small escort to block the path through Quitman Canyon, while awaiting units from the subposts. That night, he camped at the waterhole of Tinaja de las Palmas, knowing the Apaches would have to stop there for water the following day. During the night, Grierson stopped passing stages and sent messages with them summoning reinforcements from Eagle Springs and Fort Quitman. A unit from Eagle Springs arrived at 4 a.m., July 30. Grierson sent two men back to bring all available cavalry, and ordered the rest to dig in.

At 9 a.m. the Apaches spotted the troops and tried to bypass them. They were charged by ten men of the Eagle Springs unit. Skirmishing ensued and lasted for an hour, until two troops of the 10th arrived from Eagle Springs. Through misidentification, the soldiers began firing at each other, allowing the Apaches to regroup and charge. The main unit at the waterhole repulsed them, and an hour later, the reinforcements broke through. The Indians tried yet another break, but were turned back, this time to be confronted with a troop charging up from Fort Quitman. The Apaches scattered and crossed back into Mexico.

On August 2 Victorio crossed the river again, and ran into a cavalry patrol. Grierson threw a screen around the entire area, but the Indians slipped through and into the Sierra Diablos. Grierson then rushed in force to cut Victorio off at Rattlesnake Springs. The Apaches rode onto them on August 6 and were scattered by gunfire.

By late afternoon, Victorio had regrouped his men in the mountains, and had spotted a provision train from Fort Davis. The Apaches attacked, but were cut down by the escort. Attempting to fall back, they were attacked from the rear by one of Grierson's units. Shocked and confused, the Indians scattered.

Over the next several days, Grierson concentrated his troops at Rattlesnake Springs and began mop-up operations. The retreating Apaches attacked a stagecoach and killed the driver and a passenger, former General and U.S. Marshal J. J. Byrne, then recrossed the river into Mexico. For the first time in his life, Victorio had been seriously defeated.

Pressure was kept up by U.S. forces from Arizona and New Mexico, who had received permission from the Mexican government to cross the border. With increasingly fewer options, Victorio camped at Tres Castillos in Chihuahua, where he was attacked on October 14, by Mexican volunteers and Tarahumari Scouts under Col. Joaquin Terrazas. The battle raged all day and into the night, until a Tarahumari sharpshooter killed Victorio. The Mexicans then proceeded to annihilate the band. The few survivors generally fled west, where they joined Geronimo. One pathetically small band tried yet another raid into Texas, where in January 1881, they massacred the occupants of a stagecoach coming through Quitman Canyon. At dawn, January 29, the Indians' group was surprised in camp by a group of Rangers who had been assigned to Fort Davis for general law enforcement.

Within a few minutes, the shooting was over, and so were the Indian Wars in Texas.

Abandonment and Restoration

Grierson spent three years as commander at Fort Davis, leaving in 1885. With him went the black units which had manned the post heroically for 18 years. White regiments replaced them and held the fort until it was closed. By 1890 Fort Davis had gas lights, a water system, and an ice plant. But it no longer served its purpose. In June 1891 the order for abandonment arrived, and on July 31 the last remaining unit, Company F, 5th Infantry, marched down the road to Marfa, where it took the train to San Antonio. Across the road, a newly arrived rancher was building a home. He was Brig. Gen. Benjamin Grierson, who had returned to Fort Davis for his retirement.

After the Army left, civilians moved into some of the quarters, so that the post was maintained reasonably well. The property was eventually sold to Mack H. Sproul, a local rancher, who in 1946 sold it to Judge David A. Simmons. Simmons ran the fort as a resort for awhile, making sure that the buildings were kept in a reasonable state of repair. In 1961, the federal government acquired the property from his heirs and made Fort Davis part of the National Park System.

Today officers row is virtually intact, and several buildings have been refurnished to the Indian War period. Two barracks have been rebuilt as a museum of the history of the fort itself and of military activities in the Trans-Pecos. The post hospital is undergoing restoration, and several other buildings still stand in varying states of repair. Behind officers row are the foundations of the original fort, built in the 1850s. The remains of the Overland Trail are clearly visible.

Two restored barracks buildings line the parade ground at Fort Davis. Other military buildings, and those of the town of Fort Davis can be seen in the background.

IV

THE CONQUEST
OF THE PLAINS

When the United States Army returned to Texas in 1865, its organization was different from the Army which Texans had known prior to the War Between the States. The change was particularly evident with horse soldiers. Before the war, mounted troops had been classed as dragoons, mounted rifles, or cavalry, based on distinct methods of fighting. This was inherited from the European forces which had held Colonial America before the Revolutionary War.

By 1861, however, the peculiar characteristics of American warfare had made these distinctions hazy, so that in fact, different horse outfits duplicated each other. A reorganization was in order, and on August 3, 1861, Congress passed a bill combining them all into a single corps under the general heading of cavalry. Regimental numbers were assigned according to date of organization. This way, the First Dragoons were redesignated as 1st Cavalry, and the venerable Second Dragoons became 2nd Cavalry. Third in seniority were the Mounted Riflemen, who became 3rd Cavalry. To further confuse things, the old 1st Cavalry was renumbered as 4th Cavalry, having been organized after the Mounted Riflemen. The 2nd Cavalry, which had served with such distinction in Texas before the war, became the 5th Cavalry, and the 3rd Cavalry was renumbered as the 6th. New regiments were added as the need arose. These included Custer's 7th, the 8th, and the superb black regiments, the 9th and 10th.

The Army's relationship with the local population had also changed. Whereas before the war, military policy had been one of containment and defense against Indians, the soldiers now came as an army of occupation. Their mission was to pacify the white population and reestablish federal authority. Texas was not considered a state; it was a conquered province. The wily Indians were quick to recognize the situation and raided pretty much at will.

The Federal Indian Policy

The federal government aggravated the situation by its Indian policy. Part of it was based on ignorance. The policy was largely set by Easterners, from areas which had not seen Indian troubles since the Revolutionary War. These politicians were under extraordinary pressure from the Society of Friends, which, with the end of slavery, had turned its zeal from abolition to appeasement of Indians.

Safe in the East, with their copies of James Fennimore Cooper with his Noble Redman, and dreamy reports from Quaker Indian agents, the politicians viewed stories of savage depredations as highly exag-

gerated. The truth was just the opposite. No horror story could do justice to the sufferings of the Texas population at the hands of the Indians.

A more sinister problem was the Indian Ring. These were politicians in high positions who received substantial revenue from the sale of contraband—modern rifles, munitions, liquor, and such—to hostile Indians. The transactions were handled by corrupt federal agents and Comancheros—renegade white businessmen—who could not have operated without federal protection.

The Officers and Soldiers of the U.S. Army

Finally, there was the Army itself. When the War Between the States ended and the parades had faded away, the military suddenly became unfashionable. Most of the Union soldiers were actually militia or National Guard. They were largely recruited from a single area for the duration. When they were mustered out, the enthusiasm of their hometowns or counties withered away. Protection of the frontier was left in the hands of nameless, faceless professional soldiers, men with no past and few prospects. They had no hometown lobby to fight for them as a miserly Congress slashed away at the military budget. They accepted their lot, did their jobs, drew their pay, and worked at staying alive.

When the Army finally decided to regarrison the frontier, it initially tried to use the posts which had been surrendered when Texas left the Union. Those which had strategic value or which were conveniently placed were reconstructed. But there were others which had no practical purpose. These were regarrisoned on a temporary basis until new forts could be built at more advantageous sites. In the end, there were three new posts, constituting the final line of frontier defense—Fort Richardson, Fort Griffin, and Fort Concho.

With the new forts came a new breed of officer. These were young soldiers who had risen rapidly during the late war. They had been thrust directly from West Point into combat, and thus had avoided the stagnation of the Old Army. They were daring and innovative, and in most cases thoroughly qualified for their jobs. Most of them had served as generals during the war, and now held peacetime commissions as majors, lieutenant colonels, and full colonels. These were the men who took it upon themselves to pacify the plains for good. One stands far above the rest—Ranald S. Mackenzie.

Ranald Mackenzie and Quanah Parker

One of the boy generals of the Union Army, Mackenzie had been cut back from a brevet rank of major general to the permanent one of colonel after the war. Still, his grasp of tactics and his organizational ability brought him authority way out of proportion to his rank. With a carte blanche to handle the Indian question as he saw fit, Mackenzie was the virtual military dictator of the Texas Plains by the time he was 31.

Mackenzie realized that the only effective way to defeat a mobile guerrilla force such as the Comanches and their allies was with a counterguerrilla force. His troops were organized accordingly, to range far into hostile territory, hitting fast, hitting hard, and withdrawing immediately. Carrying this one step further, he reasoned that by destroying the Indian bases of operations, a war party would have no means of support for its raids. Consequently, he sought out and destroyed villages, burning dwellings, destroying food supplies, and capturing or killing livestock.

But if the whites had found their leader, so had the Indians. He was Quanah Parker, the half-white war chief of the Kwadahi Comanches. His mother was Cynthia Ann Parker, who had been stolen as a child in the Fort Parker raid in 1836. Quanah understood the whites well enough to have a profound respect for their ability to occupy and hold territory. Under him, the Comanche Wars took a new turn. No longer were Indian depredations mere robber raids, but a war of extermination, with each side determined to clear the other from the land.

Quanah's stronghold was the Staked Plains. In those days before the aquifers were tapped, the area was a vast, featureless desert. Determined to end the Comanche menace for good, Mackenzie explored and studied these plains until he could move in them as well as the Indians. But the more Quanah was boxed in, the more craftily he planned. Three campaigns ended in a draw, but with each Mackenzie had learned something new.

In the end, it was not the superior weaponry which defeated the Indians of Texas. They, too, were well-equipped with modern arms, and skillful in their use. The successful conclusion to the Comanche wars came from the iron discipline and imaginative leadership of Ranald Mackenzie. Backed by regulations which he stretched beyond any reasonable limit, protected from politicians by the Army command, he ruthlessly enforced obedience from his men and operated at will.

On the other hand, the Indians were bound to a code of debate and compromise among the tribal chiefs. This was their undoing.

By a peculiar twist of fate, Quanah Parker thrived in peace where Mackenzie did not. The Comanche chief made a quick adjustment to reservation life, became a land speculator, rancher, and financier. He later served as a federal judge for Indian affairs and was often seen in Washington lobbying for Indian rights. He died in 1911, very old and very rich.

After the wars in Texas, Ranald Mackenzie served for awhile in the Sioux Wars, then returned to San Antonio as permanent brigadier general and commander of the department. By now, he was worn out. Physically, he had always been frail, and years of campaigning along with seven serious wounds had taken their toll. His mind broke. He was given a medical discharge and committed to an asylum. He died in Staten Island on January 19, 1889, at the age of 48.

Mackenzie's main enemy during his Texas campaigns was Quanah Parker, half-white war chief of the Comanches. After his surrender, Quanah adjusted to white civilization, and had amassed a substantial fortune by the time of his death in 1911. (National Archives.)

Fort Concho

Headquarters Building is at 215 E. Avenue D, San Angelo, at the head of the old parade ground. Barracks line the north side of the parade, and officers' row, the south. There are some 20 buildings in all, 16 of which are original.

Fort Concho was one of the best-situated nineteenth-century posts in Texas. In an otherwise desolate area, it was located at the confluence of the North and Middle Concho Rivers. Fishing was good, there was lots of game, and trails coming westward converged there en route to El Paso.

Establishment and Early History

The post was founded when a detachment of 4th Cavalry from Fort Chadbourne occupied the site in the fall of 1867 as a replacement for their post. Foundations of the first building, a commissary warehouse, were laid the following January.

Fort Concho was slow in building. When William Notson, post surgeon arrived at the end of January 1868, he wrote that officers and men occupied tents, "the horses simply coralled [sic], and the comforts for every living creature the most limited in character. . . . The hospital consisting of three hospital tents, crowded and illy warmed by open fireplaces. There was no screens about any of the tents, either as protection against the prevalent 'northers,' or for decency, and the accommodation of the officers inferior if possible to that of the men."

But the post did grow and take on permanence. German artisans were brought in from Fredericksburg, and shaped locally quarried stones into substantial buildings. Although Fort Concho was never completed according to plan, within the next few years, more than 20 buildings were finished. Walls and floors were almost entirely of stone, with pecan rafters and beams. Even the post corral was made of stone. Meanwhile, San Angelo was established across the river, and provided ample diversion for the soldiers.

Initially, there were no organized campaigns against the Indians. Military activities were limited to escort duty and punitive actions to retaliate for raids. There were enough of those. In his report for February 1869, Dr. Notson noted that on February 22, a lumber train from Fort Concho was attacked by about 70 Indians at Kickapoo Springs. "The Indians were repulsed leaving one dead in our hand, and were seen to bear off several seriously wounded. The train lost one man (a Mexican teamster), killed, and two mules. Notice was received at the post within a few hours, and a scout under Lt. Turnock 17th Inf. was sent to intercept marauders. It returned after an absence of about three days having been unsuccessful . . . The skull of the Indian killed is in course of preparation for the ethnological collection of the Army Medical Museum."

If Indians weren't enough, the area had problems with white outlaws as well. In his April report, Notson noted an Indian attack on one of the mail coaches 20 miles north of Fort Concho. But in the following months, he wrote, "Circumstances have arisen since giving strength to the supposition that it was not the work of Indians but of whites, and indeed the complicity of the driver himself is suspected . . . The vicinity of the post has recently been visited by a small

The headquarters building contains a military museum, including refurnished court-martial room. The guns are original field pieces which were later converted to salute guns. The building in the left background is one of the old Army warehouses.

class of horse thieves, stealing the less valuable animals belonging to the poor squatters, trusting to their proximity [to the fort] for protection. One incident during the month looked as if more extended theft had been contemplated. For the conveniance [sic] of the Post, a lantern had been permitted to burn all night in the Belvedere of the Hospital. On one evening some miscreant fired a rifle ball through the windows, narrowly missing the light. Had the effort been successful a conflagration would have been inevitable, and it is surmised from some other circumstances, that the intention was during the confusion incident either the troop horses were to have been stolen or the stores robbed, perhaps both. The light was promptly discontinued."

The Arrival of Ranald Mackenzie

A gradual shift from defensive to offensive began in September 1869, when Col. Ranald Mackenzie arrived at Fort Concho. He organized a scouting party of 100 men of the black 9th Cavalry to investigate the area north of the post. The expedition engaged a large band of Indians near the Salt Fork of the Brazos, and fought for two days with no appreciable results. On October 10, Mackenzie sent a second party consisting of 150 men from Fort Clark and Fort Concho. It was joined on the trail by soldiers and Tonkawa Scouts from Fort Griffin. This expedition ran into a party of more than 400 Comanches. In the ensuing fight, about 30 hostiles were killed and a large number were wounded. The soldiers chased the Comanches back to their camp where they were routed. More warriors were killed, and eight women and children were captured, along with a large number of ponies. Although he had delegated command of the expedition to an officer from Fort Clark, Mackenzie was developing the tactics he would later unleash against the Comanche nation.

On January 7, 1870, Pecos Bill Shafter arrived to take command of the post, while Mackenzie remained as district commander. Indians were still a problem, and on February 18, a civilian was killed and scalped within a quarter of a mile of the post. Mackenzie and Shafter made an inspection tour of the area, and sent two scouting parties toward the Colorado. Throughout the spring, the garrison of Fort Concho was depleted as enlistments expired and no replacements came. Four major scouting expeditions were sent out in April, further cutting down on manpower. The post was regarrisoned during the summer, giving it an average strength of over 500 officers and men.

The year 1871 brought more frustrations. As Indian activity stepped up, Mackenzie was ordered to Fort Richardson, nearer the Staked Plains and the seat of Comancheria. Raids continued around the Concho area as well. Since scouting parties never seemed to find or keep a trail, the integrity of the guide was questioned. In May 1871 the situation reached the point where a picket was ordered from Fort Concho to garrison Fort Chadbourne (see Chapter 6).

In view of this, the Army Reduction Act might have seemed a disaster. But careful planning by the current post commander, Maj. John P. Hatch avoided disruption. In fact, Hatch used the act as an excuse to rid the post of disreputable elements, so that an efficient force could be built out of the remaining troops.

On September 22, a small band of Indians attacked a government contractor's train at Kickapoo Springs, capturing 118 mules and two horses. Members of the 9th Cavalry stationed at Fort Concho were already out on a scout, so two companies of the 4th were sent in pursuit, stripping the post of almost all its cavalry. This group returned after 48 hours. One of the companies then went back out and followed the trail to the headwaters of the Colorado before giving up.

Meanwhile, Lt. John L. Bullis, 24th Infantry, had been sent out from Fort McKavett with 15 mounted men to pursue the same war party. Bullis hounded the Indians until his men ran out of rations. Then they went to living on buffalo meat. He finally came into Fort Concho, having given up only when his horses were too exhausted to continue. But he had found several springs and abandoned camps, giving the Army an idea of where to look the next time a raid occurred.

The Army's efforts to seek out and destroy this band of Indians was a new twist to the plains wars. A few months earlier, in May 1871, Kiowas had massacred a wagon train and had barely missed getting Gen. W. T. Sherman himself (see "Fort Richardson"). With this, the Army recognized that the Texas Indians should be permanently subjugated. The punitive expeditions turned into organized campaigns. Their mission was to seek, engage, and destroy hostile Indians wherever they were found. The scouting forays organized by Mackenzie at Fort Concho were beginning to pay off.

The Mackenzie Campaigns

For the next three years, troops from Forts Concho, Clark, Richardson, and Griffin fought Comanches,

Kiowas, and Kickapoos. In the 1872 campaign, Mackenzie drew troops and supplies from as far away as Fort Brown. These were consolidated at Fort Concho and pointed north to join him near the mouth of Blanco Canyon. Over the next four months, Mackenzie swept the plains of Texas and New Mexico, until he found a large camp at McClellan Creek. Over 100 women and children were taken prisoner in that raid, and were sent to Concho until an exchange was arranged the following spring.

The next year brought a decisive victory over the Kickapoos (see Chapter 3, "Fort Clark"). But the Comanches and their Kiowa allies had once again left the reservations and remained lords of the plains. On June 27, 1874, more than 700 Kiowas and Comanches attacked a buffalo hunters' camp at Adobe Walls, on the Canadian River in what is now Hutchinson County. The battle raged for six days, until the Indians tired of it and scattered to harass other groups of hunters. That ended the buffalo season for the year.

The attacks on the hunters galvanized the military. The departmental commander, Gen. Christopher C. Augur declared any Indian off his reservation to be hostile. Mackenzie was named operations commander for a final confrontation. Col. Nelson Miles was ordered out of Camp Supply, Indian Territory; Col. John W. Davidson out from Fort Sill; Maj. William Price, Fort Union, New Mexico; and Col. G. P. Buell, out from Fort Griffin. The plan was to encircle the Staked Plains, cut off retreat to the reservations, and drive the tribes into Mackenzie's hands.

Picking up the 4th cavalry from Fort Concho, Mackenzie stormed through the plains, fighting his decisive action at Palo Duro Canyon in December. In 1875 Bill Shafter concentrated nine troops of the 10th Cavalry and two companies of infantry at Concho for an expedition to the Blanco Canyon area. Few Indians were encountered, making it obvious their strength had been broken at Palo Duro. Shafter turned his attentions to exploration and mapping, then returned to his headquarters at Fort Duncan. One unit was detached to complete the survey before heading back to its base at Fort Concho. This group skirmished with hostiles near the Rio Grande, but encountered no major problems.

In 1880 units from Fort Concho under the command of Gen. Benjamin Grierson served in the Victorio War (see Chapter 3, "Fort Davis"). But the death of Victorio in Mexico effectively ended the Indian troubles in Texas, and troops at Concho settled back to routine garrison duty.

Throughout the 1880s, Fort Concho was maintained, and nearby San Angelo grew. The Santa Fe Railroad came through in 1888, opening the town to the outside world. Indians had become only a nuisance and the fort was no longer necessary. On June 20, 1889, the flag was lowered for the last time. The band struck up "The Girl I Left Behind Me," and the soldiers marched out. They went straight to the depot and boarded the trains.

Abandonment and Restoration

Like so many nineteenth-century military posts, Fort Concho was on leased property. When the post was abandoned, the land reverted back to its owners. Buildings were rented or leased out as San Angelo grew, and consequently most of them exist today.

The headquarters is a military museum. Among the items on display are the tunic and crossbelt of Lt. Theodore Chadbourne, for whom Fort Concho's predecessor post was named. The tunic has a bullet hole from the mortal wound Chadbourne received at the Battle of Resaca de la Palma. The court-martial room, which served as an office when not being used for matters of military justice, has been restored and equipped to the period in which Fort Concho was in service. Mannequins represent an officer and sergeant of the 9th Cavalry.

The 4th Cavalry and 16th Infantry heritage groups make Fort Concho their headquarters, and show visitors something of army life in the 1880s. One barracks has been reconstructed and refurnished with the bedding and kits of the soldiers. Another reconstructed barracks is a museum of the development of Tom Green County. Concho Elementary School is on the west end of the parade ground. However, a master plan calls for reconstructing the old hospital building, which burned in 1910, and moving the school there. The school building will then be demolished and the parade ground will be restored.

Most of the officers' houses are intact, having been rented out after the post was closed. Fort Concho now serves San Angelo as a civic center.

Fort Richardson

A state historical park on U.S. 281 one mile southeast of Jacksboro.

Fort Richardson's place in history is assured by a single incident in 1871. This was the massacre of a wagon train that May, which led to the first war crimes trial of American Indian leaders, and to a dramatic turnabout in the military policy on Indians.

Sherman's Narrow Escape

A party of reservation Kiowas from Oklahoma had spent most of the spring raiding in the area, under the Chiefs Satanta, Big Tree, and Satank. Coinciding with this was an inspection tour of Texas posts by Gen. William T. Sherman, chief of staff, and Maj. Gen. Randolph Marcy, inspector general. Marcy knew the Indian situation, since he was the same Marcy who had conducted the inspection of Texas frontier posts prior to the War Between the States (see Chapters 2 and 3). Yet he was unable to convince his boss Sherman of the seriousness of the raids.

One day prior to the wagon train massacre, Sherman's party passed over the Salt Creek Prairie, 22 miles west of Fort Richardson en route to the post. It was spotted by the Kiowas, who were eager to attack. They were restrained by their medicine man De-ha-te, who predicted a larger party would come, which could be more easily captured. Sherman arrived at Fort Richardson unaware of how close to death he had been.

The Salt Creek Massacre

The following day, the Kiowas attacked the wagon train on the same spot on the Salt Creek Prairie, as it headed toward Jacksboro from Fort Griffin. The wagon master and five teamsters were killed outright. A sixth teamer, Sam Elliott, was tied to a wagon tongue and roasted. Five escaped including Thomas Brazeal, who made his way to Jacksboro. Being badly wounded, Brazeal was taken to Fort Richardson for treatment by Army doctors. There, he related what had happened, and a party was sent out to investigate.

The surgeon at Richardson described the scene they found. "All the bodies were riddled with bullets, covered with gashes, and the skulls crushed, evidently with an axe found bloody on the place; some of the bodies also exhibited signs of having been stabbed with arrows. One of the bodies [Elliott's] was even more mutilated than the others, it having been found fastened with a chain to the pole of a wagon lying over a fire with the face to the ground, the tongue being cut out. Because of the charred condition of the soft parts, it was impossible to determine whether the man was burned before or after his death."

Given the nature of the Indian Wars, one can assume the others were mutilated after death, to cripple their spirits as well. But Elliott was probably roasted alive. Had he been dead, the Kiowas wouldn't have bothered.

Meanwhile, a delegation of citizens from Jack and Parker counties came to Sherman, who assured them he would work to change the national military policy. From this he developed his philosophy, "The more we can kill this year, the less will have to be killed the next war . . . they all have to be killed or maintained as a species of paupers."

Back at the Fort Sill Reservation, the Kiowa Chief Satanta was questioned by Agent Laurie Tatum. He boasted of the exploit and implicated Satank and Big Tree as well. All three were arrested and extradited to Jacksboro for trial.

The humiliation of arrest was too much for the proud old War Chief Satank. A few miles outside of Sill, he began singing his death song. Then he slipped his chains and jumped the guard. He died as he had meant to, a warrior fighting to the end.

Satanta and Big Tree were sentenced to death. However, Eastern pressure groups forced President U.S. Grant to push for clemency. Governor Edmund J. Davis, a Republican like Grant, agreed and commuted the sentences to life in prison. Still under pressure from the federal government and Eastern Republicans, Davis paroled the two Indians in 1873 and the raids resumed.

Satanta was captured again in 1874, and returned to Huntsville. He committed suicide by jumping from an upper story window of the prison hospital. Big

The Kiowa Chief Santanta was one of the leaders of the war party which massacred a wagon train near Fort Richardson in 1871. Condemned to death, pardoned, and subsequently reimprisoned, he committed suicide at Huntsville in 1878. (National Archives.)

Tree was arrested the following year, and was again paroled under federal pressure. This time, he more or less honored his parole and died in Anadarko, Oklahoma, in 1929.

The Salt Creek Massacre was probably the most important event in Fort Richardson's history, but certainly not the only one. Most of the fort's 12-year existence centered around hostile activities.

Early History

Richardson was established in 1866, as one of the replacements for Fort Belknap. It was first set up near Jacksboro by units of the 6th Cavalry under Col. S. H. Starr. Early in 1867 the camp was removed to Buffalo Springs, 20 miles north. But that location proved unhealthy, and before the year was out troops returned to Jacksboro and set up the post on its present site, by Lost Creek.

Construction centered around the usual rectangular parade ground, with officers' quarters and bar-

racks on opposing sides. A substantial hospital building and morgue stood on one end, and officers' and support structures on the other. Housing was built of logs, pickets, or board lumber, as were some of the support buildings and offices. On the other hand, the hospital, bakery, guardhouse, and magazine were of stone.

One of the busiest buildings appears to have been the guardhouse. This was because of the boredom of routine garrison life, relieved only by forays against Indians, or by trips into Jacksboro. For their part, the citizens of the town were more than happy to look after the recreational needs of the soldiers, particularly if it meant parting them from their money. The place had 27 saloons, as well as a string of houses of easy virtue. The most notorious area was called Sudsville, and stood across Lost Creek from the post.

But the soldiers fought well when the time came. One routine patrol of 56 men under Capt. Curwin B. McLellan was attacked by some 250 Kiowas on the Little Wachita River in July 1870. It is ironic that the attack was led by Kicking Bird, a known pacifist. However, he had been accused of cowardice by other Kiowa and Comanche leaders, and this raid was to save face.

The battle dragged on. Although completely surrounded, McLellan's men managed to withdraw from their initial spot to a strong defensive position overlooking the river. Then, just as suddenly as they had attacked, the Kiowas withdrew. Kicking Bird had made his point.

A far more serious incident occurred on July 12, 1872, when a detachment of 26 Rangers under Maj. John B. Jones was following the trail of a war party between Fort Belknap and Jacksboro. The Rangers closed on the Indians as they were entering Lost Valley. At that point, the first war party was joined by another one, to bring the total to about 100.

The Indians scattered and tried to pick the Rangers off piecemeal. But the company regrouped and retreated into a draw in the valley, while the Indians fired on them from the surrounding hills. With 12 horses lost, Jones realized he could not withdraw. So he dug in while a messenger went to Fort Richardson for help. A squad of black troops arrived shortly before daylight, and the combined force swept through the valley at dawn. However, the Indians had since departed and all they found were a horse and abandoned weapons.

Troops at Richardson had a variety of duties in the early years. Among other things, they escorted cattle on the northern trails, where the herds were particularly subject to attack. In 1870 four companies of the 6th Cavalry were sent from the post to meet separate drives north of the Red River.

Mackenzie and the Battle of Palo Duro Canyon

Mackenzie arrived at Fort Richardson in April 1871, and remained until December 1872. It was here that he perfected the policy initiated at Fort Concho, of carrying the war to the Indians.

In the first campaign, Mackenzie led 600 troops out of Fort Richardson in September 1871, for a punitive expedition against the Kwahadi Comanches. The column forged into the Staked Plains, where war parties led by Quanah Parker and Bull Bear soon took the initiative. The Comanches made lightning thrusts at the column, vanishing before the troops could form a line of battle. Shortly after midnight October 10, Quanah's party charged Mackenzie's camp, ringing cowbells and waving buffalo skins to panic the horses. The Indians made off with 66 Army horses, including Mackenzie's own. A small detachment sent to recover them was charged and scattered by the Comanches, with one soldier killed. Two days later, a blizzard struck and Mackenzie turned his column home. En route, he chased after another band of hostiles, receiving his seventh wound, an arrow in the leg.

As Mackenzie recovered, he revised his tactics. Henceforth, he would fight the Indians on their own terms, with fast raids to achieve maximum destruction with minimal loss. He would hound the Comanches relentlessly until he destroyed them.

The first real success came in September 1872, when he destroyed the village at McClellan Creek, with only two killed and two wounded. In that raid, he captured 3,000 horses. That night, however, the surviving Comanches stampeded the horses and got them back. It was a hard lesson, and from then on, Mackenzie ordered all captured horses to be killed.

Although Mackenzie no longer commanded at Richardson when he won his great victory at Palo Duro Canyon in 1874, he led his troops there at the end of the four-month campaign. The break in that operation had come on the night of September 25, when Indians attempted to stampede the Army horses. A Comanchero was captured in the fight, and after a military third degree, led Mackenzie to the main Indian camp in the canyon. Undaunted by the hundreds of tepees, he attacked at dawn. The camp was routed and the villages completely destroyed. More than 1,400 horses were captured. Remembering his experience at McClellan Creek, Mackenzie had them all shot.

Harrying of the Indians continued until Christmas, when the troops were brought to a near standstill by mud, weather, and supply problems. His mission accomplished, Mackenzie led his exhausted troops to Richardson.

After Palo Duro, the northwest frontier was secure. Fort Richardson was no longer necessary. Orders for abandonment were issued on March 29, 1878. On May 23 the last units left the post for Fort Griffin.

Many of the remaining buildings at Fort Richardson are shown in this single view. The bakery is in the foreground.

Recent History

The Texas National Guard began using Fort Richardson in the 1920s. Battery F of the "Lost Battalion," the Second Battalion, 131st Field Artillery, was mobilized at Richardson in November 1940. Captured in Java in 1942, its members were scattered throughout Japanese-controlled Asia. Eight of the original 63 members of the battery died, most of them working on the Burma-Siam Railroad.

Today, Fort Richardson State Historical Park includes remaining post buildings, a museum (open only on weekends during the winter), a visitor's center, 40 picnic sites, 23 campsites with water and electricity, restrooms with showers, and a nature area.

One of the five original officer's houses still exists. Built in 1867 of locally cut cottonwood, it is typical of the hundreds of wooden officer's houses built in the nineteenth century Western military posts. Ironically, it is the only one of its kind left in the United States.

Barracks were picket, and one has been reconstructed. The original hospital has been restored and is now being refurnished. Also standing are the bakery, guardhouse, one of the magazines, and the commissary, although the last named building is outside the perimeter of the main park area. Members of the North Texas Reenactment Society and the Confederate Guard occasionally demonstrate frontier military life for visitors.

Persons desiring further information should write Park Superintendent, Fort Richardson State Historical Park, P.O. Box 4, Jacksboro, Texas, 76056.

Fort Griffin

A state historical park bisected by U.S. 283 about 15 miles north of Albany in Shackleford County. The post itself is west of the highway.

The Fort and The Flat

The post of Fort Griffin and the rowdy cowtown which shared its name are virtually inseparable. The Burt Lancaster-Kirk Douglas movie *Gunfight at OK Corral* wasn't too far off when it began with a meeting between Wyatt Earp and Doc Holliday in Fort Griffin. Both of them knew the town, and Earp is thought to have gone there to get Doc's help in hunting down gunslinger Dade Rudabaugh. Bat Masterson was in Fort Griffin as well. So were Pat Garrett, Big Nose Kate Elder, Poker Queen Lottie Deno and a host of others. At one point, the town of Fort Griffin—better known as The Flat—rivaled Fort Worth as a transit point for cattle and hides.

As usual, the military came first, and the town grew up as an adjunct to the post. We have seen how settlers in the area had to "fort up" for protection against Indians during the War Between the States, when the armed forces were called East. After the war, when the Army finally got around to protecting as well as occupying, four companies of the 6th Cavalry were sent to set up camp to replace Fort Belknap. The post was established on July 31, 1867, about 35 miles up the Clear Fork of the Brazos from

Belknap. A short time later, rains turned the area into a marsh and the fort was moved to the top of a 100-foot mesa nearby.

Initially, the post was named Camp Wilson, in memory of a lieutenant of the 6th. But in September 1867, Gen. Charles Griffin, departmental commander, died unexpectedly, and the following February Camp Wilson was designated as Fort Griffin.

In general, Fort Griffin was a miserable duty assignment. More than 90 structures were eventually raised at the post. Although plans called for every building to be constructed of stone, only six were. Barracks were originally picket, but were later replaced by six-man shanties, intended to be temporary, but which turned out to be permanent. Measuring 13 feet long by 8½ feet wide by 6 feet high, they had minimal space per man and even less ventilation.

The post hospital stayed busy. The cramped quarters did their part, and the problem was aggravated by lack of bathing facilities or regulations on personal hygiene. In the summer, soldiers washed in Collins Creek or the Clear Fork. In the winter, with the cold wind blowing through the cracks in the barracks, freezing temperatures and snow, they didn't bother to bathe. By 1874 the situation reached the point where the departmental commander, Gen. Augur, wrote to

Gen. Philip Sheridan that the post was unfit for human habitation. The following year, Sheridan's divisional survey said, "All the buildings are temporary structures of wood, in very poor condition, and inadequate in capacity."

Small wonder then, that the troops were ready to fight anyone—Indians, buffalo hunters, or each other. Soldiers from Fort Griffin served in every decisive campaign against Kiowas and Comanches. It was a key supply depot for Mackenzie's Red River Campaign which culminated at Palo Duro. Among those participating in the campaign were Griffin's Tonkawa Scouts. They lived near the post where their women often served as laundresses. The Tonkawa role is explained in displays in the visitor's center at Fort Griffin State Historical Park.

When they weren't in the field, soldiers were blowing off steam down in The Flat. Officers and men mixed freely in the saloons, gambling dens, and bawdy houses. Rank was put aside as they drank together, wenched together, gambled together, and sometimes killed each other. Several shootings between officers and men came out of poker games or drinking bouts.

The Flat's main industry was hides. Fort Griffin provided ready access to the buffalo ranges, and hide-hunters used it as their base. One store alone reportedly warehoused 30 tons of lead and 5 tons of powder. Given that kind of firepower, and the buffalo's natural tendency to continue grazing while his comrades are being shot down, the outcome was a foregone conclusion. During the 1877 season alone, about 200,000 hides were shipped through Fort Griffin.

But The Flat's businessmen realized that the more hides they shipped, the closer the industry came to dying. The buffalo herds were being exterminated, and the smart money was shifting to cattle. The Western Trail broke off from the Chisholm Trail below San Antonio, and came up through Fort Griffin en route to Dodge City. And as the Kansas Legislature extended its quarantine line on Texas cattle to shut off the traditional markets served by Fort Worth, more and more cattle came through Fort Griffin on their way to Dodge. In 1876 over 100,000 head of cattle passed through.

Cowtown Rivalries

Fort Worth had always prided itself as being Cowtown, even if the name wasn't yet formally applied. It was the major shipping point for anything having to do with cattle or the plains. But before anyone knew it, Cowtown had a rival. Confident in its repu-

tation and busy with its own enterprises, the Fort Worth business community didn't see the threat at first. But when it finally woke up, Fort Griffin's position was established, and Fort Worth had a serious rival.

It was 1878 before anyone in Fort Worth realized something was wrong. By then Fort Griffin was not only diverting cattle below San Antonio, but had agents in Belton, to catch any that might come through there. By the middle of the summer, The Flat had drawn off 150,000 head of the season's cattle, compared to only 100,000 for Cowtown.

The 1878 season was beyond salvage, but by 1879, Fort Worth had fielded Dave Blair to meet the drovers on the trail and talk them into coming back. They came, and Blair assured his employers that the upstart on the Clear Fork had been handled. He was wrong. Grazing on the Western Trail was better and it was still relatively free of fences. And Fort Griffin's agents made sure everyone in Texas knew about it.

Now it was The Flat's turn to be cocky. The Fort Griffin *Echo* published taunting editorials, which brought snarling replies from the Fort Worth *Democrat*. When the season closed, Fort Worth had handled more than half the cattle, but did not have a large enough margin to subdue The Flat.

The Old Law Mob

With Fort Griffin's boom came all the lawlessness that characterized the Frontier West. The military up on the hill had no real jurisdiction over the town, and as we have seen, the soldiers were often major contributors to the problem. One post commander tried to extend his jurisdiction to The Flat, but it didn't last long. Civilian peace officers were generally the type characterized by Wyatt Earp or Bat Masterson, and tended to bend the law to suit themselves. The answer was a vigilance committee—in Fort Griffin, it was called the Old Law Mob or O.L.M.

The Old Law Mob left no mistake as to who they were or what they were about. Undesirable elements were told to leave town. If they didn't, they were often found strung from trees, or dead from a sudden case of lead poisoning. The letters "O.L.M." would be written on a piece of paper pinned to the bodies. Soiled doves, card sharks, and other members of The Flat's less respectable citizenry generally moved on after seeing their names on O.L.M. advisory bulletins.

Some semblance of official law and order came when the Rangers established themselves at nearby Camp Sibley. But the real calming influence turned out to be the Army. It calmed things down by leaving. In May 1881 the government ordered the post abandoned. Fort Griffin had been founded for frontier defense, and with the Plains Tribes pacified, it was no longer necessary. The last outfit to go was Company A of the 22nd Infantry, which was transferred to Fort Clark.

Ruin and Restoration

In The Flat, the ever-industrious business community decided to weather this blow as well. A massive public relations campaign was mounted, with agents praising the town throughout Texas. This time, it wasn't enough. The buffalo herds were gone, and the cattle drives were winding down. Fort Griffin lost the county seat to Albany, and was bypassed by the railroad to Abilene. One by one, the saloons, gambling dens, and bawdy houses shut down as people moved on. The last store closed in the 1950s.

Today, one has a hard time finding any trace of The Flat, even when looking for it. The only remnant is the shell of Fort Griffin Lodge No. 489 A.F. & A.M., founded in 1877 and built of solid stone. Today, it consists of only four outer walls, with no roof, no sashes in the windows and no floors. The lodge still exists, but it meets in nearby Throckmorton.

Up on Government Hill, within the boundaries of Fort Griffin State Historical Park, one finds the ruins of the post itself. Begin the tour with a stop by the well-developed visitor center, which not only explains the history, but has a model of the fort up on its mesa and a portion of The Flat below. Just beyond the center is the gigantic, 45-foot deep well, which provided drinking water and saved Griffin from the fate of Fort Belknap. Two replicas of barracks face the main parade ground. They are open, but not recommended for anyone who suffers claustrophobia. Ruins of officers quarters, consisting primarily of chimneys and foundations are off the north parade ground. Beyond that is the sutler's store, which is one of the best preserved ruins on the post. Ruins also exist of the administration building and the magazine.

Ruins of the headquarters building, Fort Griffin.

Lord of the plains, a Texas longhorn takes his ease on the grounds of Fort Griffin State Historical Park, which houses the State Longhorn Herd.

The post bakery has been reroofed, and its brick ovens are still intact.

The park is home of the Texas State Longhorn Herd. These cattle were originally assembled in the 1920s by J. Frank Dobie in one of the first efforts to save the longhorn from extinction. Fort Griffin's herd is descended from Dobie's and is owned by the Texas Department of Parks and Wildlife. The cattle are carefully managed so that only the animals showing the truest longhorn characteristics are kept. This herd has provided seed cattle for Possum Kingdom, Abilene Copper Breaks, Palo Duro Canyon, Dinosaur Valley, and LBJ state parks. And it is the source of the various Beevos for the University of Texas. Part of the herd is occasionally sold at public auction to avoid overpopulation.

Fort Griffin State Historical Park offers extensive recreational facilities. Persons desiring further information may write Park Superintendent, Fort Griffin State Historical Park, Route 1, Albany, Texas, 76430.

V
FORT SAM HOUSTON: HEADQUARTERS, DEPARTMENT OF TEXAS, U.S. ARMY

Fort Sam Houston

Near downtown San Antonio. Fort Sam Houston can be reached several different ways. The easiest is to take I-35 to the Fort Sam Houston exit. This leads directly to the Quadrangle.

Fort Sam Houston has the distinction of surviving from the Indian Wars into the modern era. It supplied troops for the final drive against the Indians. It trained soldiers for the Spanish-American War, the Philippine Mutiny, both world wars, and the Punitive Expedition into Mexico. The roster of commanders includes such names as Edward O. C. Ord, Ranald S. Mackenzie, Frederick Funston, John J. Pershing, Walter Kreuger, Courtney H. Hodges, and Jonathan M. Wainwright. Today, it is Headquarters, Fifth United States Army, and contains historic structures from throughout its years of service.

Establishment

As we have seen, Texas military posts were supplied from San Antonio. The government rented downtown buildings, including the Alamo. After the War Between the States, the Army returned with 4,000 troops under Bvt. Maj. Gen. Wesley Merritt. Once again, headquarters and supply were downtown in the Alamo and rented buildings. In addition, barracks were constructed, although their low-lying location made them subject to two major inundations from the river, and caused general health problems.

A lady MP stands guard at the sally port of the Fort Sam Houston Quadrangle. Despite its forbidding appearance, the Quadrangle was built as a supply depot and not for defense. It is now Headquarters, Fifth Army.

Headquarters was removed to Austin in 1869, and all troops were withdrawn from San Antonio in 1873. It was during this period that the post-war Fifth Military District was broken up, and the Department of Texas was created. Initially it was attached to the Military Division of the South, but later became part of Gen. Phil Sheridan's Military Division of the Missouri.

For some time the people of San Antonio had considered donating land to keep the military in the city. This became urgent when New Braunfels offered 150 acres for the Army to move there, and especially so after the move to Austin. In 1870 the city donated approximately 40 acres in the eastern part of town, a site which later became known as Government Hill. The following year, a second site of about 40 acres was purchased and offered by the municipal government. When the military deemed both inadequate, a third site was donated, bringing the total amount up to about 93 acres. The Army accepted, and when troops returned in 1875 a temporary camp was established on the donated land, and occupied by the 3rd Cavalry.

Meanwhile, the idea of using San Antonio as a central depot was questioned by no less than Sheridan himself. He felt the Northern and Western garrisons could be supplied through Kansas and the Indian Territory, and that Forts Clark, Duncan and McIntosh could receive provisions through Indianola or Brazos Santiago. The latter port was already used for Fort Brown and Fort Ringgold. The chief of staff, Gen. W. T. Sherman agreed, as did Secretary of War W. W. Belknap.

But San Antonio wasn't finished. City officials sent Col. Thomas G. Williams, a former Confederate officer, to lobby in Washington. Despite his Southern ties, Williams had many powerful friends, including President U. S. Grant. Williams met with Sherman on January 15, 1873. He also discussed the case with Quartermaster General Montgomery Meigs, one of the few ranking officers who supported the San Antonio project. Meigs backed it on the basis of economy—a major factor with the military of the period—and ease of supplying posts with which to police the border.

Construction

Grant, in turn, supported an appropriation bill for $100,000, which crawled through Congress and came back for his signature on March 3. There were several more Sheridan roadblocks, but in the spring of 1875, Meigs notified the Department of Texas to begin work. On June 7, 1876, the government entered into contract with Ed. Braden and Co. for construction of a depot building and tower—the famed Quadrangle—on Government Hill. The base price was $83,120.25. With $15,246.37 worth of options, the final cost to the government was $98,366.63.

The Quadrangle consisted of four outer walls, enclosing 36 storerooms, 20 offices, workshops, and a cellar. Despite its fortress-like appearance, it was intended from the beginning as a depot and not a fortification. The so-called "loopholes" appearing in early photos were actually small ventilation windows, which have now been replaced with full-sized modern windows. The tower, originally designed as an elevated water storage tank, was converted into a clock tower in 1882.

Although departmental headquarters had returned to San Antonio with the rest of the troops, it was once again located in rented buildings downtown. The Quadrangle served as the quartermaster depot. As such, a vital function was upkeep of horses and wagons. Blacksmiths and wheelwrights lined the north wall. A gate at either end led to corrals, stables, and wagon sheds in back. Storerooms were along the east and west walls, with offices and the main entrance in the south wall.

In 1879 departmental headquarters were moved to the post. The following year, plans were made for 15 sets of permanent officers quarters and a temporary hospital, immediately east of the Quadrangle. These were completed by 1886 and came to be known as the Staff Post. Number 6 Staff Post Road, completed in 1881, was designated as the commanding officer's quarters and has been used for that purpose ever since. The house is shown on guides as the Pershing House, since it was used by General Pershing when he took command of the district in 1917, following the Punitive Expedition. He was living here when he was named commander of the American Expeditionary Force to France. The house is 10,800 square feet, has three living rooms, six bedrooms, and six-and-a-half baths. It is currently occupied by the Commanding Officer, Fifth Army.

The Infantry Post was built in 1886, after living conditions in the San Antonio barracks became intolerable. This was beyond the donated land, on two tracts purchased by the Army in 1882 and 1883. This became the first permanent barracks and headquarters for the post itself, as separated from departmental headquarters in the Quadrangle. Apartment E in Building No. 688, at the intersection of Grayson Street and New Braunfels Road, was occupied in 1916 by Lieutenant D. D. Eisenhower and his wife,

Mamie. Eisenhower was again at Fort Sam Houston in 1941, and lived by the intersection of New Braunfels and Dickman Roads. Here he was promoted to brigadier general.

Wartime and Peacetime

The false economy which plagued the period following the War Between the States was felt by the military in Texas as well as elsewhere. The Army tended to concentrate troops in larger posts. Subposts were maintained only when outlawry and Indian raids became so great that they could not be ignored. Since this left large areas of Texas unprotected, troops from the major forts were continually on escort and scouting duty. This included troops from Fort Sam Houston, even though it was designed and intended for supply. The end of the Victorio War in 1881 effectively settled the Indian problem in Texas, and after the surrender of Geronimo in 1886, the Southwest became quiet.

Geronimo, Naches, and 31 other Apache leaders were sent to San Antonio for detention, arriving un-

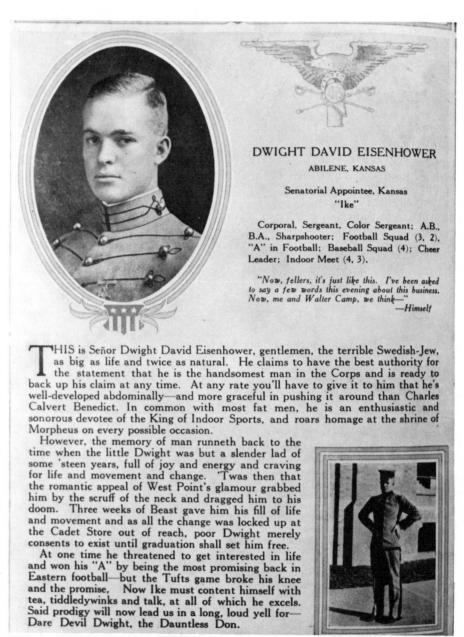

DWIGHT DAVID EISENHOWER

ABILENE, KANSAS

Senatorial Appointee, Kansas
"Ike"

Corporal, Sergeant, Color Sergeant; A.B., B.A., Sharpshooter; Football Squad (3, 2), "A" in Football; Baseball Squad (4); Cheer Leader; Indoor Meet (4, 3).

"Now, fellers, it's just like this. I've been asked to say a few words this evening about this business. Now, me and Walter Camp, we think—"
                                        —Himself

THIS is Señor Dwight David Eisenhower, gentlemen, the terrible Swedish-Jew, as big as life and twice as natural. He claims to have the best authority for the statement that he is the handsomest man in the Corps and is ready to back up his claim at any time. At any rate you'll have to give it to him that he's well-developed abdominally—and more graceful in pushing it around than Charles Calvert Benedict. In common with most fat men, he is an enthusiastic and sonorous devotee of the King of Indoor Sports, and roars homage at the shrine of Morpheus on every possible occasion.

However, the memory of man runneth back to the time when the little Dwight was but a slender lad of some 'steen years, full of joy and energy and craving for life and movement and change. 'Twas then that the romantic appeal of West Point's glamour grabbed him by the scruff of the neck and dragged him to his doom. Three weeks of Beast gave him his fill of life and movement and as all the change was locked up at the Cadet Store out of reach, poor Dwight merely consents to exist until graduation shall set him free.

At one time he threatened to get interested in life and won his "A" by being the most promising back in Eastern football—but the Tufts game broke his knee and the promise. Now Ike must content himself with tea, tiddledywinks and talk, at all of which he excels. Said prodigy will now lead us in a long, loud yell for—Dare Devil Dwight, the Dauntless Don.

Young Dwight D. Eisenhower brought his bride Mamie to Fort Sam Houston shortly after graduation from West Point. Years later, he was promoted to brigadier general at the post. (U.S. Military Academy Archives)

der an escort of Fourth Cavalry on Sept. 10, 1886. They remained for 40 days, living in tents in the Quadrangle. On October 22, they resumed their journey to imprisonment in Fort Pickens, Florida, escorted by Company K of the 16th Infantry from Fort Sam Houston.

During this entire period, the post was known simply as the Post at San Antonio. But on September 11, 1890, the War Department ordered it named Fort Sam Houston. By now, Texas was largely settled, and San Antonio had long since ceased to be a wild frontier town. President Benjamin Harrison visited San Antonio and Fort Sam Houston in 1891. There were regular band concerts and dress parades. Society maidens attended functions as escorts for young officers. So many married into the military over the years that San Antonio became known as the "Mother-in-law of the Army."

The destruction of the battleship Maine in Havana on February 15, 1898, led to a declaration of war against Spain. On April 16 Col. Louis Carpenter, commander at Fort Sam Houston, was ordered to send all available troops of the 18th Infantry to New Orleans. The following month, Carpenter himself was ordered to follow with the 5th Cavalry.

A new group descended on San Antonio for equipment and training. It was a volunteer regiment made up of tough cowboys from Arizona and the Indian Territory and the cream of New York and San Antonio. Officially, it was known as the 1st Volunteer Cavalry. Soon, however, it came to be called the Rough Riders. Its commanders were Col. Leonard Wood, a former military surgeon of the Geronimo War, and Lt. Col. Theodore Roosevelt.

The Rough Riders arrived May 7, camping and training in what is now Roosevelt Park. From then until May 30, when they left for Cuba, they managed to shoot up a band concert, and get repeatedly scattered over the drill field and parade ground by their half-wild horses. One officer watching a review toward the end of their stay said it was the worst demonstration he had ever seen.

Mobilization and supply at Fort Sam Houston continued through the Spanish-American War and the subsequent Philippine Mutiny. The latter was a short, vicious affair, the first American experience of jungle war with a basically hostile population. Among those who died was Maj. Gen. Henry W. Lawton, one of Ranald Mackenzie's officers in the 4th Cavalry. He had commanded the detail which had escorted Geronimo from Fort Bowie, Arizona, to Fort Sam Houston. His death left his family destitute and the San Antonio papers joined in a national appeal for contributions. He had been well-liked in San Antonio, and contributions were many.

During this period, there had been shifts in the military structure of the South and Southwest. The Department of Texas had been abolished on March 11, 1896, and consolidated with the Southern Department, headquartered in Atlanta. Pressure to reverse that decision began immediately, and on June 6, 1899, the Department of Texas was reestablished. Once again, headquarters were in Fort Sam Houston.

Recent History

Throughout the years, there had been considerable construction at the post as its functions expanded. In 1909 President William Howard Taft dedicated a post chapel, which due to numerous bequests became known as the Gift Chapel. Another building was erected in February 1910 as the Army's first aircraft hangar. The Army procured a wrecked Wright biplane and assigned Lt. Benjamin Foulois and a crew to rebuild it. Foulois managed to get it together and fly it to Laredo. San Antonio became air conscious, and in 1914, Kelly field was established as the first Army Flying School. It was named for Second Lt. George E. M. Kelly, killed in a crash at Fort Sam Houston in 1911.

The Revolution and collapse of law and order in Mexico brought extensive activity to the post. As Mexico continued to deteriorate, Europe went to war, adding to the duties. The first steps toward meeting the problem were taken by President Taft in 1911, when he ordered formation of a provisional division at Fort Sam Houston, made up of existing cavalry, infantry, and field artillery regiments, augmented by Signal Corps and Engineers. Then in 1916 President Woodrow Wilson ordered mobilization of National Guard units from Texas and several Midwestern states. They were billeted in an area north and east of the post. The encampment was initially called Camp Wilson, after the president, but was subsequently changed to Camp Travis for the Alamo hero. Maj. Gen. Frederick Funston was assigned to command. Camp Travis became a major training depot, and before the war ended in 1918, it had turned out 208,000 soldiers.

In addition to these activities, Fort Sam Houston had become Headquarters for the Southern Department, which included Texas, Louisiana, Arkansas, Oklahoma, New Mexico, and Arizona. It also became a general depot for all types of supplies throughout the district. Because of these developments, particularly the establishment of Camp Travis, the federal government purchased 13 tracts of land totaling about 1,400 acres for the reservation. The depot itself had to expand, and once again the Army leased property in San Antonio.

Construction continued after the war, as the Army concentrated various training activities there. The most outstanding single addition was the new post hospital, which was occupied in February 1938, and became Brooke General Hospital. Since it opened with 329 patients, it has become the leading burn treatment center in the Western Hemisphere. During this period also, the New Post with its Spanish-type architecture was constructed to replace Camp Travis.

From late 1942 until early 1944, Fort Sam Houston served as Headquarters, Third Army, under the successive commands of Lt. Generals Walter Kreuger and Courtney Hodges. The Fourth Army made it Headquarters from January 26, 1944, until June 30, 1971. Gen. Jonathan M. Wainwright received command on January 19, 1946, after his return from Japanese imprisonment, and served until 1947.

The Fort Today

Today, Fort Sam Houston is Headquarters, Fifth Army, and Headquarters, U.S. Army Health Services Command and the Academy of Health Sciences. It serves approximately 125,000 persons, including active military, dependents, retirees, and civilians. From the first donations of land around Government Hill, it has expanded to a government-owned reservation of 3,026 acres. Some 500 acres in the oldest part of the post have been declared a National Historic Landmark.

The best way to begin a tour is in the Quadrangle. Brochures are available there, providing information and tour routes. Deer, peacocks, rabbits, and ducks roam the enclosure, as they have since the 1880s. A replica of an early blacksmith shop has been set up on the site of one of the original forges along the north wall. The Fort Sam Houston Museum is in an old mess hall on S-4 Road, and covers the history of the U.S. Army in San Antonio and the Southwest. Hours are 10 a.m. to 4 p.m. Wednesday through Sunday. No visit to the post is complete without seeing it. The U.S. Army Medical Museum covers the history of military medicine since 1775. It is open from 8 a.m. to 11:30 a.m., and 12:30 p.m. to 4 p.m. Monday

through Friday, and is located on Connell Street. The museums and Quadrangle are open to the public. Officers quarters such as those used by Eisenhower and Pershing are residences and are not open, although they can be viewed from the street on a tour.

Another point of interest is the grave of Pat the Artillery Horse, who was retired when the 12th Field Artillery was motorized in 1938, and who died in 1953. Historic areas also include the Artillery and Cavalry Post, the Gift Chapel, the Infantry Post, Camp Travis and the New Post, and Brooke Army Medical Center. Memorials honor the first flight by Benjamin Foulois and Combat Medics.

The grave of Pat the Artillery Horse, who was retired in 1938 when the 12th Field Artillery went mechanized, and died in 1953 at the age of 45.

VI
OTHER FORTS

All told, the United States Army had more than 30 establishments in Texas dignified by the title "fort." Although the word denotes a permanent military installation, very few actually qualified.

For all the forts which left their names in history, there were others which were abandoned within a few years of their founding. At times, they proved unnecessary. Often, the rapidly moving frontier rendered them obsolete before they ever served any real purpose. And very, very often, they were too poorly situated for any practical purpose.

The War Between the States ended the service of some. When U.S. authority was reestablished in Texas, and the time came to regarrison the frontier, the Army used the opportunity to build posts in more advantageous positions. Regardless of how they were abandoned, the forts generally deteriorated until little, if anything remained.

In the present century, military establishments are located on declared reservations, which have been purchased and are owned by the federal government. When such installations are declared surplus and abandoned, the Department of Defense tries to find some suitable public use. Priority generally goes to educational purposes. Such was the case of Fort Brown, Fort Ringgold, and Fort McIntosh; they became schools. Municipal uses get secondary consideration, followed by public health. Fort Duncan went to both. The installation is offered to private bidders as a last resort. This was the case with Fort Clark.

Things were different in the nineteenth century. The federal government rarely purchased the land on which the posts were located. In Texas, where private property is the rule and public lands a rarity, posts were built on rented or leased land. In some cases, even the buildings were rented. Rarely was a permanent reservation declared. So when a military installation was abandoned, the land simply reverted back to the property owner.

Some fort sites have been obtained by the state, by a city, or by a county, in an effort to preserve at least some small portion of the past. Some exist as ruins, but on private property. Others have buildings still standing, but which are utilized by the property owners. Some have vanished entirely, leaving only their names to adjoining towns or the surrounding counties—or leaving nothing at all.

Fort Chadbourne

On private property, visible to the east of U.S. 277, about 10 miles north of Bronte. Not open to the public.

Fort Chadbourne is another of the "Lee forts," visited by the future Southern general at various times during his tours of duty in Texas. It was founded on October 28, 1852, as part of the string of posts protecting the advancing line of civilization from Kiowas and Comanches. It also occupied an important point on the Overland Trail. Initially constructed of picket posts set into the ground, it was rebuilt in stone. It is the ruins of these solid, though deteriorating structures which are visible today.

The post depended on Oak Creek for water, and this was never reliable. In fact, water and Indians remained a major problem throughout the post's existence. Relations with Indians varied. Comanches showed up from time to time, and one Comanche woman who begged bread from the garrison always wore a bonnet. She was Cynthia Ann Parker, covering her light hair to conceal her true race.

During periods of boredom, soldiers would race horses. One time, they were thoroughly fleeced by a group of Comanches who encouraged them to bet heavily against a none-too-impressive-looking Indian mount. When the race began, the Comanche pony took the lead, and left the soldiers behind in a trail of dust, much poorer for the lesson.

The Comanches could turn against the troops at a moment's notice. Soldiers returning late and liquored up from a night at the Dutchman's saloon were sometimes waylaid while crossing the creek.

But the soldiers could pay in kind. When two Army mail carriers were captured, tied to trees and burned to death, the post commander, Maj. Seth Eastman summoned tribal leaders to Fort Chadbourne and put them under arrest. In the ensuing scuffle, ten of the chiefs were shot, nine by infantry who had been drilling in the background as a precaution, and one by Lt. C. W. Thompson, as the chief tried to hold out at gunpoint in an officer's house.

Abandonment

Like other U.S. installations, Chadbourne was abandoned during the War Between the States, although there were brief periods of Confederate occupancy. Because of its location on the mail route to El Paso, the post was regarrisoned by Company G of the 4th Cavalry on May 25, 1867. Within two months, there were 331 men at Fort Chadbourne, but because of water shortages, the occupation was temporary until Fort Concho was established. From then on, it was used sporadically as a sub-post of Concho, during the early years of that fort.

William M. Notson, the ever-observant post surgeon, noted that when he arrived at Fort Concho in January 1868, Company A was on detail to Fort Chadbourne. The following month, the picket was relieved and sent to Fort McKavett, although it was reestablished shortly thereafter. One of Notson's associates, an assistant surgeon named Dumreicher, was detailed from Fort Concho to serve the garrison at Chadbourne, "and wound up his relationship to the army, by being cashiered under sentence of Gen. Ct. Martial in June."

Notson noted several other pickets sent to Chadbourne from Fort Concho, until his report for April 1872, when he wrote, "The permanent picket at Chadbourne was discontinued and the Medical officer stationed there, returned to the Post [Fort Concho]."

Finally, on April 16, 1872, Notson wrote, "Actg. Asst. Surg. R. Gale rejoined the post from his picket station at Chadbourne." Fort Chadbourne was abandoned for good.

Today, the most visible ruins are those of the two stone barracks and two of the officers' houses. Most of the other buildings exist only as half-buried foundations. The post is located on Chadbourne Ranch, about 100 yards from the main office. While I received total cooperation from the ranch management during my visit, it should be brought out that Chadbourne is a working cattle ranch and not a tourist attraction. The serious student would do best to call the ranch from Bronte, to determine whether it is convenient to visit. The public can read the Fort Chadbourne historical marker on a rise from U.S. 277 overlooking the post, and visit the nearby cemetery.

Ruined barracks, Fort Chadbourne.

Fort Elliott

Near Wheeler is the old town of Mobeetie, site of Fort Elliott. This was the last of the frontier posts of Texas, established in 1875. Oddly enough, it was in the Department of the Missouri, rather than the Department of Texas. This was due to its location north of the Red River, which made it more useful for duty in the Indian Territory and Kansas. It was supplied from Fort Leavenworth, instead of San Antonio. Troops from Fort Elliott helped police the Cherokee Strip during the Land Run.

The fort was constructed almost entirely of wood. No visible trace remains.

Fort Ewell

One of the least-attractive duty assignments in the early years of the Indian wars, Fort Ewell was established in 1852, to cover the road between San Antonio and Laredo. It was abandoned two years later, as the site was unhealthy.

The post was some 40 miles southeast of Cotulla. Such traces as remain are across the Nueces from modern roads, denying easy access to the casual visitor.

Fort Fisher

In Fort Fisher Park by Lake Brazos in Waco. Take the Fort Fisher exit on I-35.

Fort Fisher was one of the string of Ranger posts projected by the Republic of Texas to defend the frontier. It was established in 1837 and named in honor of Secretary of War William S. Fisher. However, it was shortly abandoned as being too remote.

The present reconstruction includes barracks and support structures facing a parade ground, the whole surrounded by a low wall. It houses the Texas Ranger Hall of Fame, the Homer Garrison Memorial Texas Ranger Museum, and one of the best firearms collections in the state. One portion of the building is also headquarters for the Ranger company assigned to the Central Texas area.

The Ranger museum is well worth anyone's time. It traces the Rangers in legend and reality from the earliest days, going so far as to examine the image presented by Hollywood and comic books. Its overall appraisal of the Ranger Force shows the bad as well as the good. Such honesty in their own museum

shows the Rangers for the great organization they are.

Fort Gates

Near present-day Gatesville was another of the original line of posts, established in 1848. Fort Gates was active until 1852, but today, only a marker denotes the big post, which once sprawled east of town.

Fort Graham

Reconstruction in Old Fort Park at the end of FM 2604, about seven miles northwest of Whitney.

Fort Graham was part of the original line of frontier forts between Fort Duncan and Fort Worth. It was founded on April 17, 1849, and named in honor of Capt. L. P. Graham of the 2nd Dragoons.

The post was about a mile east of the Brazos. In 1851 Col. Samuel Cooper, assistant adjutant general of the United States, used the post as base for an expedition upriver to check on the Indian situation. After inspecting the villages on the Upper Brazos, he filed a report listing the needs of some of the tribes and assessing the possibilities for additional military posts. The following year the Legislature began procedures which led to the establishment of the Young County reservations, near what would become Fort Belknap (see Chapter 3).

Two of the groups Cooper found were Shawnees and Delawares. "They had recently been moved to this place from the neighborhood of Fort Graham on account of the recent department orders which require that Indians found within the line of military posts shall be put to death," he wrote.

Two years later, on September 10, 1853, Bvt. Lt. Col. W. G. Freeman inspected the post as part of his departmental survey, and found it in sad shape. In fact, he reported, "Orders had been received to abandon the post and the movement was delayed by the want of transportation. Much of the Company property was boxed up in readiness for the march." Apparently there had been some trouble at the post, since Freeman noted Fort Graham had been commanded by Bvt. Maj. R. A. Arnold, "but three days before my arrival he was killed by the Asst. Surgeon of the post and I found the command exercised by the next in rank, 1st Lt. R. H. Anderson, 2nd Dragoons." Unfortunately, he offers no more detail.

Fort Graham was abandoned shortly after Freeman left, and fell into ruins. In 1936 a barracks building was reconstructed on the original site by the Texas Centennial Commission, and served for many years as a community meeting place. However, in the 1970s, the level of Lake Whitney was raised 13 feet, subjecting the fort site to frequent flooding.

Local citizens organized the Fort Graham Restoration Committee, to relocate and reconstruct the building. Funds were raised, the barracks was bulldozed and such stones that were still serviceable were used in the reconstruction on higher ground.

The replica was dedicated as an area museum on May 31, 1985. The museum is open from 10 a.m. to 3 p.m. Saturdays, and 1 p.m. to 5 p.m. Sundays. Long-range plans call for reconstruction of other post buildings at the new site.

Fort Hancock

Fort Hancock is a settlement on I-10, some 70 miles east of El Paso. The fort itself was established in 1882, as a sub-post of Fort Bliss, and remained active until 1895. Some traces remain near the river, but none of particular note.

Fort Inge

Fort Inge near Uvalde was the second of the original chain of federal posts built in 1848–49. Founded in 1849, it was occupied off and on until 1869. Gen. Lew Wallace began work on his novel *Ben Hur* here.

Several years ago, there was some talk of restoring the post. To date, though, no serious action has been taken. The land has been cleared, and a few traces are visible over the site, which is noted by a historical marker. However, there is nothing of any particular interest.

Fort Leaton

On FM 170, four miles southwest of Presidio.

Originally founded by the Spaniards, Fort Leaton passed into private hands and was never a U.S. Government post. But its history of frontier violence and intrigue make it equal to any fort in Texas.

The post was established by Capt. Alonso Rubin de Celis in 1759, as the Presidio of San Jose. The Spaniards maintained a garrison until 1767, when the site was abandoned in favor of one across the river. With no military protection, the empty post was destroyed by Indians. In 1773, the Spaniards reoccupied San Jose, and maintained a 50-man company into the early 1800s.

The fort had been empty for about 30 years when Ben Leaton wandered out of the desert in 1848. A former bounty hunter who had collected Indian scalps for the governments of Sonora and Chihuahua, Leaton bought the ruins and rebuilt them into a fortified hacienda. This served as the center of a vast farming operation, as well as for a trade monopoly with Apaches and Comanches. The latter enterprise brought accusations from the U.S. and Mexican governments that Leaton encouraged Indian raids into Mexico by trading for stolen livestock. But soldiers who came through were won over by his lavish hospitality and an outwardly charming disposition.

Ben Leaton lived in his fort from 1848 until his death three years later. His widow married Edward Hall, who ultimately went into debt to John Burgess, one of Leaton's friends from scalphunting days. When Hall defaulted, Burgess foreclosed. In the ensuing disputes, Hall was murdered and Burgess moved into the fort.

Eleven years later, Burgess was murdered during a trip to Fort Davis, by Hall's stepson, Bill Leaton. However, the Burgess family remained in the fort until 1926.

After it was abandoned, the fort deteriorated. Although attempts were made to restore it, Fort Leaton was largely a ruin when it was donated to the state in 1968. The fort originally contained more than 40 rooms around a central plaza. Twenty-five rooms have been restored, and are open to the public as a historical museum from primitive times to the present.

Fort Lincoln

There are no remains of Fort Lincoln, founded in 1850 near D'Hanis.

Fort Martin Scott

This fort was established in 1848 near Fredericksburg, to guard a frontier which soon outpaced it. By 1853, it had shrunk to a 19-man forage depot.

Like Fort Inge, there is occasional talk of restoration, but nothing has developed yet. There are no noteworthy remains.

Fort Mason

In Mason, about five blocks south of the Mason County Courthouse, at the end of Post Hill Street.

Little is left of Fort Mason now, except for a marker and one reconstructed officer's quarters built on original foundations. However, it was once a key post in the chain of forts protecting the frontier, with 23 permanent buildings. It was also Robert E. Lee's last field command as an officer in the United States Army.

Establishment

Fort Mason was established by Bvt. Lt. Col. W. H. Harvey of the 2nd Dragoons on July 6, 1851, on a site selected the previous year. It was named in honor of Lt. George T. Mason of the 2nd Dragoons, who had been killed in a skirmish near Brownsville on April 25, 1846. By the time of the oft-mentioned Freeman inspection of 1853, the post had field and staff officers, a band, and two companies of dragoons.

"The presence of the regiment band tends greatly to enliven the post and render the men contented," Freeman wrote in his report. "It is required to play daily at the stated periods for the entertainment of

A reconstructed stone officer's house is all that remains of Fort Mason, Robert E. Lee's last command as an officer of the United States Army.

the command, and on such occasions groups of soldiers may be seen seated peaceably in front of their quarters and listening to the music with evident satisfaction."

During this period, the post was commanded by the fiery Col. Charles May. This didn't last, however, since Fort Mason was abandoned on January 25, 1854. With the military gone, Comanche and Apache raids stepped up. The following year, Col. Albert Sidney Johnston was ordered to take 750 men of the newly organized 2nd Cavalry from Jefferson Barracks, Missouri, to Texas. Johnston made Mason the regimental headquarters, with six companies.

Indian Skirmishes

Troops from Fort Mason had numerous skirmishes with Indians. The most notable began in July, 1857, when Lt. John Bell Hood set out with a patrol of 24 troopers in seach of a reported Comanche war party. After 12 days, the patrol located a fresh trail and began pursuit. Sixteen days later, the trail showed the original band had been joined by a much larger party.

Finally, the soldiers encountered a group of Indians who met them with a white flag. Although this was an invitation to parlay, Hood didn't trust them. Just as he suspected, the Indians dropped the flag and opened fire at 20 paces. More rose up from hiding places around the soldiers, and attacked with gunfire and arrows. Yet another group rode into the platoon and began a vicious hand-to-hand fight.

The soldiers emptied their revolvers, then began hacking away with sabres. Hood caught an arrow in his left hand, but continued to fight. Finally, the Indians set fire to the grass and scattered to avoid concentrated pursuit.

Hood's casualties totaled two dead and five wounded. After burying the dead, the patrol rode to Fort Clark, where Hood filed his report before returning to Fort Mason.

The patrol, which had originally been planned for about 3 days, lasted 5 weeks and covered more than 500 miles. The men had run out of food early on, and had existed as best they could off the land. It later turned out the fight had involved nearly 100 Comanches and Lipan Apaches. Figures of Indian losses vary, but Hood estimated 10 killed and 12 wounded.

Closer to home, troopers from Fort Mason frequently engaged local Lipans and Wacos. In 1859 one company is said to have used camels from Camp Verde to chase down a Comanche raiding party. This was a test to see how the imports would do under actual combat conditions. There is no record of whether hostiles were encountered, but the camels seemed to have performed well.

The Command of Robert E. Lee

During this period, the post had undergone several changes of command. Col. Johnston had been ordered to San Antonio in April 1856. Fort Mason then had various commanding officers until December 1860, when Robert E. Lee arrived to take charge of the 2nd Cavalry.

The quiet, cultivated Virginian encouraged social events and entertainment. Relations grew between him and citizens of the nearby town of Mason. Dances were held in Lee's honor, and he in turn hosted events as the occasion arose.

In the East, relations between the federal government and the South had broken down, and several of the Southern States had withdrawn. The news filtered out to Fort Mason, where on January 23, 1861, Lee wrote the letter to his son which contained the

The historic marker at Fort Mason reads like an honor roll of Union and Confederate officers. The Second Cavalry, headquartered at Mason, provided a superb training ground for officers on both sides of the War Between the States.

famous passage, "If the Union is dissolved and the Government disrupted, I shall return to my native State and share the miseries of my people, and save in defence will draw my sword on none."

A short time later, Lee received orders from the War Department to report to the chief of staff, Gen. Winfield Scott in Washington by April 1. On February 13, he left for San Antonio. Texas had already left the Union, and while Lee was in transit between Mason and San Antonio, Gen. David E. Twiggs surrendered U.S. military property to the state. On March 29, Fort Mason was turned over to local authorities.

The fort was used sporadically by Confederate and state troops, and by local minutemen called up to protect the frontier. After the War Between the States, Fort Mason was reoccupied by two troops of the 4th Cavalry. But by now, the post was no longer necessary. On March 23, 1869, Fort Mason was permanently abandoned. From then on, Fort Mason served as a quarry for local citizens, who dismantled its building for stones for the town.

The Fort Today

Aside from the one reconstructed officer's quarters, nothing remains of the fort except foundations concealed by the brush on Post Hill. The officer's quarters itself consists of four rooms, two on either side of a "dog run" hallway. The two front rooms are a small museum, dedicated largely to the fort's most prominent soldier, Lee.

Fort Quitman

A monument on the grounds of Hudspeth County Courthouse in Sierra Blanca traces some of the history of Fort Quitman, which was located about 16 miles to the southeast.

No trace of the adobe post remains today, and even the replica at I-10 and FM 34 has fallen into ruin. However, the courthouse itself is interesting, being the only active courthouse in the United States built of adobe. Be sure to observe all speed limits while in the vicinity of Sierra Blanca.

Fort Terrett

Fort Terrett filled a gap between Fort Clark and Fort McKavett. However, its position near present-

day Roosevelt was hardly strategic, since McKavett, only 30 miles to the north, was on the main military road, while Terrett was not. Although it was abandoned in 1853, much of the post is in good condition, having been built of stone, with many buildings used by the current property owner.

Uribe Home

The fortified ranch houses built in Zapata County during the Spanish and Mexican periods have almost all been covered by Falcon Lake. An impressive exception however, is the old Uribe home, built in San Ygnacio in the 1830s by Blas Maria Uribe. This is a walled compound enclosing an open square, with entry provided by a gate on the west end. A sundial set over the gate in the 1850s is still in place.

The Uribe home was designed to provide refuge for the local population in the event of attack by Indians. It survives as a prime example of a structure which was as much a fortress as a residence. It is occupied and is not open to the public. However, visitors may walk around the outside walls.

San Ygnacio itself is little changed from the colonial period. It served as one of the locations of the Marlon Brando film *Viva Zapata*. The town is located on U.S. 83, 35 miles southeast of Laredo. An interesting local museum is maintained on the school grounds.

Military Camps

Although not designated as permanent posts, several sites of camps are worthy of mention.

Camp Verde, between Kerrville and Bandera, was headquarters of Jefferson Davis's Camel Corps. The old camel khan or corral, copied in every detail from those used in the Arab World, has disappeared. But other buildings remain, albeit on private property.

The 1857 cantonment of Camp Wood is at the town of the same name.

Nothing is left of Camp Hudson, although there is a marker on State 163 in Val Verde County.

The roll of long-vanished posts goes on and on. Fort Merrill, Fort Polk, Redmond Ranch, Indianola. They have vanished and are forgotten. Forgotten by everyone except the shades of the soldiers who served them.

Index

JA 06 '95	DATE DUE		
APR 20			